G. W Hely-Hutchinson

Reminiscences of the Lews

Or, twenty years' wild sport in the Hebrides

G. W Hely-Hutchinson

Reminiscences of the Lews

Or, twenty years' wild sport in the Hebrides

ISBN/EAN: 9783337312855

Printed in Europe, USA, Canada, Australia, Japan

Cover: Foto ©Suzi / pixelio.de

More available books at **www.hansebooks.com**

REMINISCENCES OF THE LEWS;

OR,

TWENTY YEARS' WILD SPORT IN THE HEBRIDES.

BY "SIXTY-ONE."

With Portrait of the Author and Illustrations.

LONDON:
BICKERS & SON, 1, LEICESTER SQUARE, W.C.
1873.

[*All Rights Reserved.*]

ERRATA.

Page 15, line 18, *read* Muzzy *for* Muggro.
,, 57, ,, 11, ,, lulled *for* beguiled.
,, 97, ,, 11, ,, above *for* about.
,, 107, ,, 8, ,, and then *instead of* so then.
,, 111, ,, 13, ,, and when they *instead of* I.
,, 115, ,, 2, ,, in my dissertation.
,, 162, ,, 4, " the " *to be omitted.*
,, 204, ,, 4, *read* Mansell *for* Watson.
,, 205, ,, 17, ,, see *instead of* pree.
,, 214, ,, 19, ,, lice *for* hue.
,, 217, ,, 13, ,, glittering *for* glistering.
,, 223, ,, 7, *omit* " that he."
,, ,, ,, 15, *read after* fire Latour Maubourg or Poniatowski.

TO

FREDERICK MILBANK, ESQ., M.P.

MY DEAR FRED,

PRIMUS INTER PRIMOS in all Noble Sport, to you I dedicate these Reminiscences, in memory of the happy days spent with you and yours in the Lews.

"SIXTY-ONE."

CONTENTS.

CHAPTER I.
INTRODUCTORY .... *Page* 1

CHAPTER II.
PROSPECTING THE LEWS AND THE CALLERNISH INN 10

CHAPTER III.
ALINE 23

CHAPTER IV.
THE HARRIS LOCHS AND A WORD ABOUT DOG-REARING 36

CHAPTER V.
OUR FRED AND HIS HEAD NURSE 49

CHAPTER VI.
OUR FIRM AND THE WHALES 67

CHAPTER VII.
SOVAL SHOOTING AND OLD TOM'S PEDIGREE... 80

CONTENTS.

CHAPTER VIII.
SOVAL FISHING AND ARTIFICIAL SPATES ... *Page* 97

CHAPTER IX.
LOCH TRIALAVAL AND THE YOUNG GEESE ... 115

CHAPTER X.
DICK BURNABY AND GROUSE THE FIRST 126

CHAPTER XI.
DEAR OLD SHIPPY 137

CHAPTER XII.
SETTERS AND WET CRAWLS..................... 148

CHAPTER XIII.
A TAME STAG 163

CHAPTER XIV.
THE WOODCOCK AND HIS WAYS, AND SHOOTING HIM IN THE OPEN 170

CHAPTER XV.
WOODCOCKS AGAIN 187

CHAPTER XVI.
LEWS CLIMATE AND MIDGES 192

CHAPTER XVII.
STORNOWAY .... *Page* 199

CHAPTER XVIII.
SUPERSTITIONS 222

CHAPTER XIX.
M'AULAY'S STORIES............................ 233

CHAPTER XX.
MY FIRST WILD BOAR.......................... 243

CHAPTER XXI.
THE LATE DUKE OF ST. SIMON 260

CHAPTER XXII.
CONCLUSION 264

TWENTY YEARS'
REMINISCENCES OF THE LEWS.

CHAPTER I.

INTRODUCTORY.

AND so it's all over; and, like the M'Gregor, I am landless—or, rather, shooting-quarterless. I must bid adieu to the home of twenty years, to seek another, and begin the world again—old, worn out almost, but tough still.

They might as well have let me linger out the two or three years the old legs would have carried me still, and left me and my doggies in peace. But that was not to be. I had spent years in turning a bad shooting into a good one; I had tried to civilise, as much as in my power lay, the district in which I lived. I was not hated by the surrounding inhabitants. But, then, I could not afford the vastly increased rent demanded for my own creation; and so I vacated my quarters for some more opulent successor. And sorrowful indeed was my departure, and the parting with the friends of those twenty years. The companions of the wild sports of those outlandish countries become your friends and associates; and you can venture to make them so, for the Highlander is a gentleman at heart, and never forgets his respect for you, so long as you respect yourself. Besides this, if you have ever killed a stag, a salmon, or an otter in his company, you stand well with him for the rest of your days. There were also other remembrances that bound us much to one another, which, though nothing to the world, were much to ourselves. As, then, keepers, and stalkers, and gillies wrung my hand as we drank the parting "morning" together, I felt there was truth in that grasp—nay, even in the tear that stood in the eye of some, and certainly in my own. It was agony, I own, to leave that desolate home; and when I reached the hill-top, from which I caught the first glimpse of that long-loved cottage, like the Highland woman, I sat me down and cried. But, as I said, it is over; and what is to be done through the long dreary days, now that I can no longer live upon the hopes and prospects of my annual migration to my wild home ? I will try and recollect the past, and solace myself with giving some of its reminiscences, collected from notes, and journals, and game-books kept during some twenty shooting seasons passed there. They will be truthful, for it is a land with too many charms, not only for my perhaps too partial recollection, but for every true sportsman, not to be able to bear criticism and truth; and those only who do not or cannot appreciate its true worth, will feel any soreness at the remarks I may at times make upon its failings.

My record, I fear will be dull, stale, and unprofitable; for, my occupation having gone, the heart to write has gone with it. And why is it that I love that far-off land so much ? Certes, not for its beauty; for of all the dismal, dreary countries that man ventures to traverse, commend me to a great part of the Lews. I do not think that, if I wished to pick a monotonous drive, I could find anything to surpass that from the Butt of Lews through Stornoway, and for some distance on towards Harris. When the different hills of the Park, of Uig, and of Harris begin to open, the country gradually becomes more mountainous and beautiful. But all the northern portion of the island is one succession of peat, hags, and moss, studded with innumerable freshwater lochs. Of course, Lews being an island, or rather peninsula, you have always in the sea, when you see it, a noble feature; and therefore the western coast, with the broad Atlantic breaking on it, is a sight to see. The Minch, too, when the weather is fine and you can see the mainland hills, is beautiful.

But speaking of the interior portion of the northern part of the island, it presents no fine features, though you often get from it striking views of the outlines of the distant hills. My shooting-lodge was about seven miles from the commencement of the hills, and a more dismal, dreary little place you would never wish to behold. I do not think you would have found many people to live in it when first I took it. There was sorry accommodation for the quality, scarcely any for servants. It was under a hill, and it looked out on the peat stacks only, which were ranged where they were cut in the peat bog; for, with the greatest possible ingenuity, the builder of the mansion had managed that from no window except the skylight at the top of the house could you contrive to get even a glimpse of a rather pretty loch close by. All that separated you from the peat stacks was the high road to Harris. Certainly, then, our situation was not picturesque; and yet, lover of beautiful scenery as I am, and having at times sojourned in very lovely spots (once for years at the head of the upper lake of Killarney—and show me anything much fairer than Gheramene), I would rather own that little cottage on the roadside looking out on the peat-stacks, and live and die there, than pass my life on the Lake of Geneva, somewhere near Chillon, among a constant succession of fine sunsets. But then there is no accounting for tastes, and tastes are formed in odd ways. It is, however, time that I should get on to narrate how it was that I ever got to this queer little place.

I was sitting one morning in June, 1850, at Borthwick Brae with F. M. and R. M., when Snowie's list of shootings came in. Among the advertisements was one of some shooting in the Lews and in Harris. Long, long ago my old friend, the late Sir Ronald Ferguson, a grand old soldier and a first-rate sportsman, recommended me to go and try those parts, as being alone compatible with my pocket and my views of boundless space to roam over. I had often tried to get those two men, F. M. and R. M., to join and take some country in those far Hebrides, but I was perpetually laughed at for talking about what did not exist, and answered with the slang of the day about imaginary things, "which it is Harris." Throwing the paper over to F., I exclaimed, "Now will you believe?—Look there!" And lo! there were three shootings in the Lews advertised (which, with Harris, forms that island dignified with the name of the Long Island), with a reference for further information to a gentleman in Edinburgh. The spaces seemed large, the rents small. Accordingly, instanter the phaeton was ordered to the door; to the nearest station we drove, and were in Edinburgh in time to find our gentleman at home. He was perfectly fair. "You had better go and judge for yourselves. If you expect to get Highland grouse-shootings, you won't. If you can walk, you may kill some few brace daily. You will get plenty of stalking, but the deer do not run large, and their heads are small, and might be stolen out of the mainland heads and not missed. You are not to expect fine Highland streams and large salmon. You will only find small streams, but plenty of fish in them, though not large. But, as I said, go and judge for yourselves. The next steamer for Stornoway sails on Thursday, and if you can get down to Glasgow to-morrow you will catch the *Mary Jane,* and get to Stornoway on Saturday. Stay there a week, fish as much as you like, and make any inquiries you please. Look at our game-books and judge for yourselves; but if you take anything there and afterwards don't like it, don't say you were done." Accordingly we took that straightforward gentleman's advice; and I have often and often thought of his words when experience taught how perfectly accurate they were. We went back home for a few traps and our fishing-rods, and started for Glasgow the next morning, whence we sailed in the *Mary Jane* northward, ho!

Reader, are you fond of the sea? Do you love dancing in a cockle-shell over the blue sea-lochs of the north-western coast of Scotland? If so, sail or steam from Dumbarton to Stornoway; and if you have the steamer a good deal to yourself, without too many passengers—children in particular—without too many sheep or cattle, or any other incumbrance, and with fine weather (all things of not very frequent occurrence), if you do not enjoy it, stop at Glasgow the rest of your life. Down the Clyde by Arran, and round the Mull of Cantire, with a strong tide and half a gale of wind meeting each other; and across to Islay, and then up the Sound of Jura, and so on to Oban; then through the sound of dark Mull, into quiet Tobermory, round Ardnamurcan Point with a good south-wester and the Atlantic tumbling in upon you, to Egg and Rum. Fetch up at Armadale, and look into the sea-loch opposite to you, running up into the mainland. Then onward up the Narrows of Skye, diverging now and then into some of those sea lochs on the mainland side of your course, amongst the most beautiful—if not *the* most beautiful—scenery in Europe. Then proceed, softly rippling your way round those glorious Chucullin Hills that, as you pass, ever assume some fresh fantastic grouping, until you reach that safest harbour of refuge, Portree, into which I have at times been pitched by the most fearful of squalls. There dine, fortify yourself with a strong sneaker of good cold whisky-and-water, aiblins two, light your pipe, and then across the Minch to fair, soft Gairloch; round into Ullapool and other lochs along the coast; then into Loch Inver the magnificent; and if you are not satisfied with it, and the Sugar-loaf Mountain, and the Assynt Hills in the distance, you are a man hard to please. Then set your head straight for the Long Island, and tumble across the Minch again with a good mild north-easter, if there is such a thing, into Stornoway; and having taken a look at its quiet harbour and its nice white-looking amphitheatre of a town, turn in; and if, as I said before, you are not satisfied with what you have seen, and also with visions of salmon and sea-trout, and deer and grouse, as you lie your head on your pillow, go home to your friends at once, and never again venture to pollute the fair North with your presence.

CHAPTER II.

PROSPECTING THE LEWS AND THE CALLERNISH INN.

IT was a fair, beautiful Sabbath morn, that first day of my acquaintance with the Lews; but I confess we did not make the use of it we might have done. All I did was to go on shore to call upon Captain Burnaby, then commanding the party of Royal Engineers employed in the survey of the island, to inquire about his father, who had come up with us in the steamer, and had suffered horribly from sea-sickness all the way. And if the visiting the Lews had been productive of no other pleasure than the great intimacy that took place between myself and Burnaby, deep indeed would be my gratitude to the said land. More of this hereafter. I was not struck much with anything about Stornoway except the smells. We were then about the end of June—the heart of the herring-fishery season. It was very hot and dry weather, and those acquainted with the mysteries of herring-curing can imagine the balmy odours proceeding from the curing-houses and their accumulations. If you wish to sojourn in the town of Stornoway, do not choose this particular season of the year for doing so.

Monday morning came, and with it the factor—or rather, as he is grandiloquently called, the Chamberlain of the Lews,—arrived, John Munro M'Kenzie, the model of his class, a straightforward gentleman, as sharp as a needle; not to be outwitted, and no outwitter. His name will long be remembered in those parts. He has long been removed to another sphere of business, where, I am happy to hear, he is doing well for himself and his family. With him we started to prospect the shootings. First we tried the northern, or Gress quarters, as they are called. I cannot say much for the drive to Gress, or for the romance of the scenery. Whenever you come across the Minch, that and the mainland hills beyond it form a beauty of their own; but the island here of itself is not beautiful. Gress House stands well over the sea bay, but it was then a dirty hole; though I believe now it is much improved. I remember well a discussion about the rent of the house—£50 per annum—between M'Kenzie and the then proprietor, being cut short by F. M. saying, "I would not take £50 per annum to live in it." There was an end of that shooting, though it is of great extent, and a good deal of grouse ground; five or six good stags were to be got there then, if properly managed. There used to be some very good snipe ground on it, and a nice little river—the Gress—which, when in good water, had plenty of sea-trout and some salmon. So we returned back to Stornoway, and the next day, or the one after, started again to prospect the Soval and Aline shootings.

Soval is about nine miles from Stornoway—the lodge, I mean. This is most unfortunately situated for the shooting—as, indeed, Highland lodges often are, and the accommodation was then so wretched, so totally inadequate to our wants, that we declined it at once; though in other respects it might have answered, for there were many things about it we liked. But more of Soval hereafter.

We proceeded on to Aline, twenty-three miles from Stornoway, at the extremity of the Lews, and on the confines of Harris. Then, indeed, as we advanced farther up, or rather down, the country, and neared Harris, it improved in appearance—extremely so from the time Loch Seaforth opened, and the grand panorama of the Park and Harris hills expanded. The lodge of the Aline shooting stands over Loch Seaforth, looking down towards the Minch, on the bounds of Lews and Harris, and of a soft summer's evening, on a fairer or more lovely spot never did the eye of man rest. The sea-loch, without a ripple, at your feet; Glen Scarladale's dark side, falling down upon its shores; and Cleisham towering into the evening mist, with the peaks of Langan Glen and the other Harris hills clustering round, form a scene that often and often have I passed hour after hour looking on, and thanking God for such a sight and the power of enjoying it. There are parts of the south-west of Ireland—Kerry, to wit—scarcely to be surpassed in beauty; but Loch Seaforth, on its proper day, has, in my eyes, no rival. The scene had the same effect on my two comrades, and before we retired for the night it was decided that, as far as the Lews was concerned, it should be Aline or nothing.

But then here came a difficulty. The authorities were very anxious to let the north shooting, or Soval, but wanted more or less to keep Aline—and no wonder. The Park, which was part of the Aline shooting, though it was not a forest—for it was let as a sheep-farm—

had plenty of deer upon it. There were deer, too, on Lewid and Carneval, the hills adjoining the lodge. The grouse shooting—if the disease, of the existence of which we were duly informed, had not done mischief—was fairly good. There was good sea-trout fishing, with occasional salmon, in the different lochs. The lodge—for Lewis lodges—had some sort of accommodation. Altogether, as things went, it was the best thing in the island. They offered us Gress and Soval shootings on the most moderate terms; indeed, we might have had them for what we chose to give. But we stuck to our text, and took Aline for seven years, specifying for certain things to be done there before we took possession, and while this was doing R. M. and I were sent to the Callernish Inn, there to locate ourselves and fish the Grimesta river and lochs and the Blackwater. F. M. having business on the mainland, returned thither.

It was a queer place that said Callernish Inn, then—the dirtiest little den it was ever my misfortune to locate in. With the exception of the inns in Stornoway, and one small house at Dalbeg, it was the only caravanserai in the Lews. It was an exertion to hold on to the hard, slippery, black horsehair chairs; the beds not inviting; the food, when you arrived without notice, not of the first order. The mutton —generally good in Scotland—what Highland mutton where they smear hard can be—an outward sort of thick rind, like that of a wild boar, with a thin layer of fat between it and the all but invisible lean that adheres to the bone, and that thin line strongly impregnated with the taste of the smear. But it is of the chickens I have the strongest remembrance. We had a couple for dinner the day of our arrival. We tried our hands and teeth on one: no impression. The next day, the remaining untried gentleman was sent out for our luncheon. We tried him cold, with the same success as the day before. We handed him over to the Highland keeper, who, after various futile endeavours, passed him on to Snow and Muggro, our two dogs. They had been refusing porridge in disgust for days, and, though half famished, could not break up that singular bird. But for a cold lobster (and that none of the best), I do not know what would have been the consequences of that particular day.

Fortunately, we caught plenty of sea-trout. In all Highland inns there are eggs and good preserves, and in this there was a wonderful servant, who made all those curious compounds called scones, that alone are made in the North, from meal, or barley, or flour, or Heaven knows what. A female was that servant, and she was the only one about the premises that ever seemed to me to do anything. She was both housemaid, parlourmaid, and washerwoman,—nurserymaid and lady's maid, too, for she was sister to the hostess of the inn, who was generally occupied a great part of the year in either producing or nursing babies. Poor, dear Mrs. M'Leod! I was nearly the death of her in one of the frequent visits I afterwards made to her house. Her husband insisted on my prescribing for her one night when she was very ill, and the doctor had not yet arrived from Stornoway, sixteen miles off. Among my various reputations in the country, I had one—that of being a good medico. She was writhing with pains in the stomach, and I prescribed the hottest of brandy-and-water. Fortunately, my patient rebelled against the mixture, and, in the meantime, the veritable man, dear old Dr. Millar, arrived, and prevented the absorption of any stimulant, which, in her state, would probably have killed her; and I was forbidden to practise—upon females, at least—in future. And yet, with all its drawbacks, many is the happy hour I have passed with Burnaby in that small parlour. It was a delightful fishing station. The Grimesta lochs and river were about two miles off, to the mouth of which you rowed up Loch Roag; the Blackwater river about the same distance.

The Grimesta, with its different lochs, take it all in all, is the best fishing in the Lews for sea-trout; and the different salmon-casts in the lochs, where the stream runs from one to another, are very good. The river itself, between the first loch and the sea, I never thought much of; for, though you may, and do, catch fish in it (by fish I mean salmon), yet, as a rule, fish do not rest in these short, rapid rivers. Indeed, except in very full water, there is not depth enough for them to lodge; and, generally speaking, fish do not take while running—at least, I never found them do so. I attribute the superiority of the salmon-casts in the Grimesta lochs to those of any of the other lochs in the Lews, to their being supplied with a very large body of water, as they form the outlet of the extensive and fine Loch Langavat, that receives all the waters of that side of Harris that run into Glen Langan; and the Grimesta has this advantage, that there is spring fishing in it, provided the weather is not

C

too cold, and there is no snow on the hills or in the water. By spring fishing, I mean that you may catch fresh salmon in the Grimesta in the spring—not kelts or foul fish, of which you may catch any number, if you choose to devote yourself to such ignoble diversion. Why it has this superiority I cannot say, only that it has it. I have caught three or four spring fish in a day in the Grimesta.

In the Blackwater, two miles from it, I never caught but two spring fish in twenty years, and in the Laxay I do not think I ever caught a dozen spring fish in the same space of time. I am no great believer, from experience, in spring fishing anywhere, though no doubt it does exist; but there is none, that I could ever find, in the Lews, except the Grimesta. The Laxay I believe to be a very early river, and the fresh fish there begin running in December, or at any rate by Christmas, just as they did in Killarney; and the run of salmon is over by the middle or latter end of March. Sea-trout are plentiful in the Grimesta, but they do not run large—not so large as in the lochs in the Park—nothing like so large as those in the Harris lochs, which are the best I have ever seen. At the time that I am speaking of, Hogarth had the net fishing of the

Island of Lewis, and his bag-nets had effectually done their work—so effectually that, at the expiration of that season, he begged to be allowed to give up his lease, as he had fished out the island, and would be a heavy loser if held to it. This resignation the proprietor wisely and generously accepted; but, as far as salmon were concerned, the mischief was done. I do not think that, during the month we were at Callernish, we killed above three or four grilse. The Blackwater, about two miles off, attached to the Soval shooting, we never tried, as it was very low; and Hogarth's fishermen—and no men knew better—assured us there was little use, for they thought there was not a single fish in the river. However, more hereafter about the Blackwater, as it passed into my possession when I took Soval.

The fishing in the Grimesta lochs is of course mostly done in boats, which to many is a great drawback, the generality of anglers preferring river fishing from the banks to loch fishing in a boat. No doubt, the endless varieties of a river are most captivating. You may, if you like, fish a loch from the shore; but I do not like it. Fish generally lie in a loch along the shore on which the wind blows; at least, sea-trout certainly do, and grilse, and very often, particularly if it is blowing hard, very close in shore. Now, if you cast from the shore in the teeth of the wind, to a certain extent your fish rise on a slack and bellied line, not the best form in which to hook them effectually. Having learnt the casts pretty well in many of the Lews lochs, I went to some expense in building out piers to command the different casts; but, somehow or other, I never did much from them or from the shore. But, then, I do not pretend to be anything but an enthusiastic—I never was a good—fisherman; and I must say this, that about one of the best and most successful I ever saw in my life, Sir James Matheson's piper, never fished a loch but from the shore, and always laughed at me and my boat, and nobody knows the quantity of fish he has killed in his life. I myself, despite this celebrated man's opinion, confess to being very fond of dancing about in a small coble, well held by a good oarsman, who knows the casts and how to hold his boat to them, which is all the battle, otherwise your line is slack over every rising fish instead of taut. And for wildness, I think of a rough day, in a wild mountain loch, with plenty of squalls, the rush of a fish and the bringing him to bay are no trifling excitement, particularly if the fish are game. I have had harder fights with a good 14 lb. fish in the upper lake of Killarney than ever I had with a river fish; but, then, those said Killarney gentlemen were the gamest fish I ever had to do with. Surely, however, this will be conceded, that it is wilder sport fishing a loch than a river in a boat, and there are many rivers that in places can only be fished from a boat. All this, however, is matter of opinion. In my experience of Lews fishing, fish fight much harder in the lochs than in the rivers; and for a very simple reason—the rivers are so small and narrow that fish have no room to rush and run about. In the lochs they have; in neither, however, are they very combative. As a rule, too, the fish do not run large, or, rather, did not run large; though of late years, owing to my plan of introducing artificial floods, they have much increased in size. Also, wherever rivers run much through peat moss—and in the Lews they run through nothing else—I have invariably remarked that fish, after they have been a few days in the fresh water, get dull, and have no fight in them.

But to return from this long digression. We remained about a month at Callernish, where we disported ourselves indifferently well, and then left it. Poor dear old dirty place! As a hostel it exists no more, and in its stead a very comfortable one has been built at Garrynahine, some two miles on the road to Stornoway, and kept by an excellent host and hostess, Mr. and Mrs. Morgan, who put you up well and comfortably at very moderate rates.

CHAPTER III.

ALINE.

BY this time the improvements had been, or were said to be, completed at Aline, and thither did I betake myself alone, R. M. having gone over to the mainland for some shooting.

Before entering upon life in the Lews, it would be as well perhaps to take the opportunity of saying something about the events that had taken place in that country a few years previously to our location there, and which were at that time sowing a seed that was hereafter to bring forth much fruit. I do not want to enter into a history of the Lews—how the Fife lairds took possession of and held it—how they gave place to the M'Kenzies. Suffice it to say that some six or seven years before our arrival, the present owner, Sir James, then Mr. Matheson, bought it of Mrs. Stuart M'Kenzie, of Seaforth; and a very fortunate purchase for the said country it was, for he had just returned from China with his pockets full of gold, and, not knowing well what to do with it, lavished it broadcast on his newly-acquired property. The potato crop failed, and the famine took place two or three years after he came in. The new proprietor had the means of keeping his people alive, and right magnificently did he do his work. Though he may eventually have got back some part of the large sums he had advanced for food, in labour on his numerous buildings and improvements throughout the country, yet—honour to whom honour is due!—but for Matheson, the Lewisians would have starved (there was no poor-law then), and deservedly should he have his niche among the benefactors of mankind. Besides this, he made roads where none were before, and opened the country. By great outlays he established regular steam navigation between Lewis and the mainland, thereby, alas! making its existence known—which then it was not—to an inquisitive public. By putting on two steamers of his own, he made a trade, which, when given up by himself, Glasgow was willing to take up. He built a very good slip for the building and repairing of vessels. He built a good, commodious castle, and kept constantly at work a large body of the Stornowegians in the various works and improvements about it.

He introduced gas; and, though last, not least, a good system of agriculture; he set up a good model farm himself, and did what neither here nor hereafter will he ever be forgiven for—he drained and converted into good land the best snipe ground in the country—viz., that round Stornoway. Well and worthily, then, has he merited the baronetcy the Government gave him, the very year, I think, we reached the Lews. But yet, with all these claims to respect, the proprietor lacked one quality. Having passed the chief part of his life in the East as a diligent and successful man of business, he was ignorant of everything connected with sport; he held sportsmen in no very high estimation, considering them as eminently selfish. He fell into the very common error of thinking that, because they were well acquainted with their own subjects, they must consequently be profoundly ignorant of all others. In fine, he kept a bountiful good mansion at a bountiful good rate, was as hospitable as a Highlander, and, when kindness was wanted, as open-handed as he was kind-hearted.

I arrived, as I stated, at Aline by myself, and came in for a very cheery, exciting scene —by way, I presume, of welcome. There had been a long-vexed question pending between

Lews and Harris—the decision of the boundaries. It was now drawing to its close. The Dean of Faculty (afterwards Lord Colonsay) and several of the Scotch lawyers concerned in this suit—pending since the Deluge—had gone round to Loch Raisort to mark the ground, accompanied by the pointers-out of both boundaries from the respective countries, and by my friend, Captain Burnaby, and his sappers, the Chamberlain, and a host of people.

A steamer had also been sent up to accommodate many of the party, and the said vessel was well laden with good viands and liquors for their creature comforts. And pleasant indeed were those Scotch lawyers—when were they otherwise than capital company? Lord Colonsay to great legal knowledge added the deepest insight into the good qualities of a deerhound of any man I ever met; and from him I got a cross of his famous dog that was the model for the hound that lies at Sir Walter Scott's feet in the Memorial in Edinburgh. I was younger then by many years, and had an Irish story or two for them that tickled their fancies, and a pleasant night we passed. There were pipers, of course; and how they danced, despite all the anathemas of the Free Kirk!

Each party danced his best for the honour of his country and of the boundary he had pointed out and sworn to, and which, I do verily believe, would have been given in favour of Harris but for too much proving. An old patriarch swore to some cinders placed years ago by his ancestors as a landmark, but which turned out to be the remains of a fire lighted there by the sappers some four months back. This was, as you can conceive, damaging.

Next day I sent such of the lawyers as could fish to do so whenever they liked, and Burnaby and I went to Loch Larcastal, a loch in the Park, to get at which we had to row across Loch Seaforth, and then walk about seven miles, a stiff pull over the shoulder of Benmore; but the loch is a good one, and the sea-trout run large. It was a good hard day's work.

Next day Burnaby went. I was left alone in my glory, and, like Robinson Crusoe, had time to look over our possession and consider its real capabilities. Our sport consisted of deer-stalking, sea-trout fishing—for there were but few salmon—and grouse shooting. Our ground was not forest, though the Park (part of our ground) would, if the sheep were taken off, make a very beautiful forest. It is a large tract of country—almost an island; for Loch Seaforth on one side, and Loch Erisort on the other, run very close to one another at high water. It contains over 75,000 acres—some very fine hills for deer, with excellent feeding-ground, and its venison is the best in the Lews.

In former times, in the time of the M'Kenzies, the late Lord Seaforth tried to make a forest of the Park by building a wall across from Loch Seaforth to Loch Erisort, to keep the deer in; but this had long ceased to exist. But the great drawback to the Park then was, when it was part of the Aline shooting, that between the house of Aline and it lay Loch Seaforth—a beautiful, picturesque object in fine weather, but in bad—which it sometimes can be in those latitudes—not the pleasantest place in the world to cross, except in a very good sea-boat, manned by four good oars and a good coxswain. There were days in which it was no pleasant work getting there or back, and this passage was a great damper of sport. Moreover, there was in the whole of this Park but one small bothy, in which the sportsmen, gillies, and stalkers could put up—and what a den it was! I never shall forget the first day we got there—wet, of course. I

ALINE, LOCH SEAFORTH.

had shot over, R. M. had stalked. The roof let in the rain, the floor was earth; more smoke came into the room than went up the chimney. But we were tired and hungry, and turned soon into those holes in the wall called, *Scotticè*, bed-places. In the morning—it had rained all night—the floor was an epitome of the Lews—land dotted with lakes; and, I remember well, we had to get turf creels or bits of old planks to lay down like hearthrugs by our beds, to step on as we rose. But what will not deer-stalkers go through? Then, too, we had the best and gamest stalker I ever knew, and the most honest and plucky of men. Long may you live, Murdoch M'Aulay, and may I be spared, as they say north, to kill another stag with you, and that this year!

I must stop here a moment to mention an instance of M'Aulay's pluck. An individual with whom he was stalking knocked a stag over, and M'Aulay went on to cut his throat or bleed him. The animal, to all appearance dead, jumped up and pinned him against a bank by a burnside. He had just time to seize the animal with both hands by his horns, and being very strong in the arm, and with his back to the bank, held it at bay. He called out to the slayer of the deer to come on and stick the animal with his knife, that had fallen in the struggle; but the cautious gentleman—shall I call him such?—had no intention of so doing, but kept tickling and infuriating the already sufficiently-enraged beast by sundry pokes and prods behind. M'Aulay, seeing this, interfered—" If you can't do better than that, stop, or I shall be killed; for I can't hold out much longer! Put my knife on the bank close by me, with the haft towards my hand, and get out of the way!" With great difficulty the hero was induced to approach near enough to do as he was told. M'Aulay then, watching his opportunity, let go one hand, seized his knife, and buried it in the stag's heart. I never asked him whether he ever stalked again with his gallant comrade.

Murdoch is a first-rate boatman—cool, and knowing his work well. Look at him running down steep crags after a wounded stag, and you will almost shudder for his neck; and if you are in for a scrimmage out of which you cannot get, look over your right shoulder, and be sure you will find M'Aulay close up.

Lewid and Carneval, the hills just above Aline, were good hills for deer, but they also were under sheep, and of course liable to constant disturbance from the shepherds, who are always doing something with those pests of all sport—Highland or Lowland—gathering or driving them for some purpose or other. You are also very much dependent for your sport on these two hills upon the terms on which you are with the tenant of the Harris shootings. The boundary line between Harris and Lewis running just across Lewid, you cannot, in certain winds, stalk it without the permission of Harris to go into their ground to get at it. Fortunately, we were ever on the best of terms with Harris and its shooting tenants, and received from them every permission that could assist us in our sport in any way. We had their permission to fish their lochs—the best I ever came across—and shoot their woodcocks in their fine glens. Many and many pleasant days have I had with those "forays into Harris," as we used to call them.

With this permission, we found Lewid and Carneval very useful stalking hills—close at hand, and, therefore, very convenient; commanding fine views of Loch Langavat and Glen Langan, and looking across to the proprietor's forest of Kenrisort, into which we anxiously peered. Woe betide the good stag that came out to see the world on our side!

There is one great drawback to the stalking of the Lews. The stags are not fit to shoot—at least as far as heads are concerned—till at least a month after the mainland. The velvet, as a rule, is never off the horn till the very end of August, and rarely completely till the middle of September—at least, that is my experience; and though you may shoot stags till the middle or 19th of October (though their necks swell long before that), yet, taking the lateness of the season and the climate into consideration, the stalking season is both late and short. Of course there are the hinds, and, as far as skill goes, every one knows how much more difficult those fit to kill are to stalk than stags; yet few, I should think, would care much for stalking, if there were nothing but hinds to shoot.

Our fishing was almost entirely loch-fishing; for though there were short streams running from Loch Georgium and Loch Stroundavat to Loch Seaforth, we scarcely ever got fish in them. Sea-trout were caught, and good ones, in these two lochs, but seldom salmon —why or wherefore I never could make out, for there were fish. There were also in the Park the Skipnaclet Lochs, the Eischkin Lochs, and Loch Larcastal—to my mind, the best loch in the Lews for large sea-trout. All three, however, were difficult of access from Aline, and it was an expedition to reach them; but still I managed to get sport in them. Now, however, that the Park shooting is taken away from Aline and made into one shooting, and a good lodge built in it, all this fishing is more accessible.

The grouse shooting we expected not to be very first rate, as the grouse disease was in the island. But I did not expect, nor do I ever remember seeing, so large a space of ground so utterly denuded of game. Grouse, as every one knows, are later the farther north you go. I had shot in Ross-shire before, and the birds are at least a fortnight later there than in the more southern counties. In the Lews, as a rule, I do not hesitate to say that, though you may shoot grouse at the beginning of September, they are a month later than the mainland birds, and should not be shot before the middle of September.

I never, probably, shall forget my essay at grouse shooting in the Lews. I shot from Aline to Balallan Bridge (seven miles) with good dogs, and during my progress killed three birds (all I saw), and those three scarce fit to pick up. R. M. and I shot another day together, walking miles, and only finding six birds, which we killed for the sake of the dogs. Poor things! they fairly gave up the ghost, and demurred to hunting.

Never in my life before or since do I remember such a shooting season. There was actually nothing to shoot over the whole of our ground, containing about 130,000 acres. We killed this year—two guns, R. M. and myself—seventy-six brace of grouse. Moreover, I shot over the whole of the adjoining Soval shooting, containing some 75,000 acres, and killed on it about thirty-five brace more. Had I not seen it, I would not have believed that disease could have created such havoc, and we began to despair of grouse shooting, at least for the seven years' lease we had just taken.

It is also fair to state there was another reason to account for the small amount of grouse to be found at that time in any part of the island of the Lews I then shot over. As I mentioned before, the survey of the Lews was then going on, and parties of Burnaby's sappers were stationed all over the country, in either tents or huts. Few of these quarters were without one gun, one fishing-rod, and one good terrier, at least. Of course they made good use of their leisure hours, and, though their commander looked after them to the best of his power, they poached like fury—at least, they were great fools if they did not. What, then, with the disease and the survey, which went on till 1853, the shooting tenants had not a blooming time of it; and we often thought and talked about the hardship of putting the country to great expense in surveying such a place as the Lews. I believe that afterwards the land survey was of service to the Admiralty survey of the sea-coast, which was indeed a blessing to those navigating these seas. Be this, however, as it may, never anywhere that I have shot did I see so little to be got as at Aline. I spent the whole winter there, and my diary records the most minute entries. The weather was atrocious, such as one must have inhabited those latitudes to comprehend. There were very few snipes or woodcocks, and the only sport I got during the year was when I went down to Stornoway to stay with Burnaby, and shot with him. The best snipe shooting in the island was about Stornoway, very often near the town, and within five to nine miles' distance round. Grouse, too, did not seem to have suffered so much in those regions as about us. Altogether, as far as sport was concerned, my first season in the Lews was not cheering.

CHAPTER IV.

THE HARRIS LOCHS AND A WORD ABOUT DOG REARING.

I WAS disappointed with the first winter I spent in the Lews. I had expected to see many wild things there, but noticed few. Of eagles, gulls, hawks, ravens, and crows, there were plenty, and some martin cats; but I had expected numbers of wild-fowl, in which I was mistaken. There were ducks and teal, occasionally wild geese (these last breed in the island). I have heard of wild swans, which are occasionally shot, but never saw one. From the lochs, on which the wild fowl are, being very open, they are hard to be got at. Snipes and plover breed in the country, but generally leave it towards the middle or end of October. Some remained, and many came over from other parts to those more northern and western. Golden plover breed largely there, and abounded on the north and west; but, though a famous bird to eat, I never saw much pleasure in that sort of shooting. Woodcocks generally do not arrive in flights till the first or second week in November, though I have shot them early in October. Strange to say, though they breed largely on the adjacent mainland, I never knew an instance of their breeding in the Lews. As there is no wood in it, all the woodcock shooting is on heather. Particularly good dogs are wanted to find them; and both you and your dogs must have a very accurate knowledge of where to look for them. A really good woodcock dog ought never to forget any spot in which he has ever found a woodcock. Certainly, the first year of my sojourn I found very few; but then, perhaps, I did not know where to look for them.

Some parts of the Park had a great reputation, and justly so, for cocks; but then there was Loch Seaforth to get over, and the winter days were short, and not so serene as one would have wished. I got through this first dreary winter, as I said, very much disappointed, for I never was in any place where there was so little to shoot or to do, and the weather was so vile, that once I remember being all but confined to the house for three weeks; but I solaced myself with the idea (a fond one) of spring fishing—alas! it was but an idea, for there was no spring fishing to be got—unless you call catching kelts and foul sea-trout fishing: I don't. The streams held brownies, or brown trout, doubtless; but when you did get them, they were not worth carrying home; and I formed then the opinion that I have ever since adhered to, that, except in the Grimesta, there is no such thing as spring fishing in the Lews. And I do not think the fish come into Loch Seaforth before the middle or latter end of July, if so early.

As the summer drew nigh, F. M. and his family, and R. M. came up, and the former brought with him a little yacht, schooner-rigged, which we flattered ourselves was to be of the greatest service in taking us round into the different sea-lochs in the country for fishing, shooting, and stalking purposes. The *Heather Bell* was that little craft named; and never were men so deceived as we were in her useful capabilities. She had a skipper who was a tolerable carpenter; also an able-bodied seaman, as he styled himself, and we called him "John of the Yacht"—the most arrant poacher that ever stepped: he used to shoot deer with slugs on his way home and back Saturday evening and Monday morning, to pass his Sabbath. The gillies and our forester occasionally served as crew, and but for the latter, the sole serviceable seaman of the lot, I believe we should have come to grief. With no wind that blew could this useful vessel get out of our loch, and if she ever did get out, she never came back again for months. F. M. once took his wife a cruise in her, and, coming back, was glad to land on a rock in the middle of the loch, where he would have been now, but that, fortunately, R. M. and I were shooting in the neighbourhood, and our boat was drawn up on the shore, with a gillie in charge, who descrying the party, relieved them from their position and took them home. After this event, F. M. only embarked his own precious person in this sylph of the waves. Did he attempt taking her anywhere stalking, the odds were he had to land where best he could, and make his way across country to his ground. She looked pretty from the windows of the house, and that was all the use she ever was to F. M., who, after keeping her for two seasons, sold her for less money than he paid for the cables he furnished her with. She never was of any use to any one but the skipper and " John of the Yacht," who both saved money enough out of their wages during the time she was in service to take them out to Australia, where they did well. One lesson I learnt from her, and that was, that no yacht is of the least use in those parts that is not a steamer; then one is most useful. Indeed, if I had the world to begin over again, and had a shooting in one of those far-off regions, I should never bother myself with a land establishment, but make my ship my home, keeping my dogs on shore.

I remained three seasons at Aline, passing my time most pleasantly; but certainly, at that time, though there was ground,. there was not game enough for three guns. The ground got up slowly to be what it was when F. M. performed his great feat of killing one hundred brace of grouse to his own gun in one day. It was not all at once that the improvements made began to tell. There was then neither road nor path across the Park, and really the stiff walks across the hills there, either for fishing or shooting purposes—for each day's sport there necessitated an expedition entailing crossing Loch Seaforth—were not repaid by the sport obtained. F. M. had not then made a good walking-path for nearly four miles up to Benmore, which greatly facilitated operations there; neither had he so increased the size of the house at Aline, and so improved it in every way, that it became a much more comfortable residence.

At that time, too, if ever man was insane on the subject of fishing, I was, and Aline did not afford me the salmon fishing I pined for; therefore, in 1852, I took Soval for myself, because it then possessed two salmon rivers. I did not, however, remove there till 1853, and I have often wondered how my legs carried me through that same year, 1852.

One of these two salmon rivers, the Laxay, was about twelve miles off; but I did not much care for it, as, till doctored by me afterwards with artificial spates, it was little worth. The other river, the Blackwater, was distant, I should say, fifteen miles good—seven along the road, and then eight across the muir—perhaps more, a strong walk, with a ford or two to cross, that in good fishing weather was not low. I used to start early and walk to it, fish all day, and go on to sleep at the Callernish Inn, three miles off, and reverse this home the next day. Then, also, I stretched my legs, in order that they might not stiffen, backwards and forwards, between our place and the Harris lochs, that were some seven or eight miles off—a stiff walk, but it was worth it; for what lochs they were! Loch Scoost, with its high peak above you, that you almost feared to walk under lest it should fall and crush you; Loch Vosimit, with its rocks and little islands, the grandest loch I ever threw line in; and Loch Ulavat, with its overlapping eagle's cliff and cavern; and all three with such awful squalls that you had hard work to hold on, particularly if standing on a rock up to your knees in water, fighting a salmon, or two big sea-trout on at the same time.

Oh, the happy, glorious days I passed in that fairyland of fishing among the Harris lochs! No wonder the legs have felt and suffered for it, and are stiff and feeble now, and call out, "Hold! enough," as I stumble, and blunder, and potter over fallows and stubbles. But the dog has had his day, and, if he is used up, you cannot take his day back from him, and he will still whine and dream over it—ay, and more than that, if I visit those parts again, which I hope to do, I'll put a charge on the old legs, and they shall carry me, God willing, another season yet into those fine glens.

A curious thing happened on one of those long walks. I was returning from Loch Vosimit, where I had been fishing one very hot day, and narrowly escaped drowning, the boat I was in choosing to fill with water and topple over; and no wonder, as her seams had been opened by the sun. Fortunately, she chose the immediate vicinity of a little island for this exploit, so my gillie and I scrambled on to it, none the worse, and not even wetting our luncheon, which we discussed on it, and then sorted our boat, which held water better after submersion. I was returning home, when I lost my *prospect* (Scotch name for telescope) —without which I never stirred—out of its case. I retraced my steps, but it was past our finding. I was sore vexed, for it had been my father's, and was knocked out of his hand at the Battle of Eylau by the bursting of a shell, which killed his horse, but did no further damage to him than a slight scratch on the nose. I tried every means of recovering it in vain. At last it was found, nearly two years after, by one of Burnaby's sappers—strange to say, none the worse after cleaning, though it had been out in the open, caseless, for two winters; and I have it still, and a very good clear glass it remains.

When in these diggings I learnt, or rather perfected, a lesson on dogs and their ways, that I had studied a good deal before; and I shall say a little about that lesson here, more particularly as public attention has lately been called to it in the *Field* by the discussion between W. C. and "Idstone," as to the point of—in broad terms—breaking dogs to what they are wanted for. I have always held W. C.'s opinion. If you want a grouse dog, break him on grouse; a partridge dog, on partridges; a snipe dog, on snipe; but I think you want more than this. You must break a dog according to the country you shoot in, for here what is sauce for the goose is not sauce for the gander.

For the first year or two that I was at Aline, F. M.—than whom no better sportsman and shot at everything exists in Europe—used the same team of dogs he had brought from the south. They were an excellent lot of pointers, very well bred, very handsome, and perfectly broken. I had shot over them on the Yorkshire moors, and in the border counties of Scotland, and they were perfection. In the Lews the whole lot were not worth five shillings. They quartered their ground in the most scientific manner; but they might have quartered it to all eternity and done no good. Their range was not high enough; they were not wild enough for ground on which there was then but little to find, and the poor animals gave up the thing in despair. F. M. soon found out this, saw it would not do, sent his pointers back to England, where they were as good as ever, and took to setters and a different style of breaking. I did the same, though I always kept one or two of my old pointer blood. It was poor "old Tom's" first season then, and he was early trained to gallop hard and range wide for his game, which I think the pointer with a cross of foxhound in his blood will do better, more judgmatically,—ay, and longer,—than any setter I ever saw. I then, for the remaining time I spent in that country, took special care not to break my dogs there as I would for English, or Perthshire, Aberdeenshire, or other lower Scotch moor ground; in fact, not to overbreak them. Obedience, of course; perfect stanchness, backing, down-charging; but I left their range alone. With dogs that have to gallop miles, perhaps, before they come on grouse—which in that country are most migratory in their habits—if you kept drawing your parallel lines you would make very small progress indeed. Therefore, when I saw my dogs, on whom I could perfectly rely, making their casts, I never played on the flageolet to them, but let them make it, and well was I repaid for the confidence placed in them. True, you could not let the grass grow under your feet; but they stood for ever, you got to them at last, and birds generally lie well in those northern regions. R. M., who shot with me my last season of the Lews, as he did the first, and who knows a dog as well as most men, did not like their desperate range at first, and exclaimed, "Where are they going to?" But he came to, and owned it was the proper breaking for those parts.

I remember well, one fine evening, poor old "Whack," a pointer, was let off, and he took one of those sweeps that no dog I ever saw could surpass. The beat was a large flat, running down to a loch, round by its side to a river, along its banks, and then up to the higher grounds above it. I had taken up a position where I could watch his movements. He scoured the plain, tried the lake sides, down by the river to the pools, and swept by me up the glen to the hill tops. I should be afraid to say what was the distance Whack traversed in that wonderful cast, but it was miles. Back came the old dog down the glen to me. "Got them at last, master, but I have had a hard gallop for it. Let me fetch my wind—a sup of water—and now come along, and we'll have a good evening's sport." And so we had. The good old dog had at last found the line of birds —the flat at the head of the burn—he took us to them, and we were well rewarded. Now, with ordinary ranging dogs this never could have been done; yet this very same Whack, the first time I took him out in a civilised country, in Yorkshire, where there were clouds of unapproachable grouse in a small compass, was useless. In about half an hour he came to me, and said, "I'm no use here; I don't understand this, and if you please I'll keep at heel." And so he did; and when at last, by a fluke, I or some one else killed a grouse, he retrieved it, for he is a perfect retriever of winged game. After laying it carefully at my feet, and turning it over and over in every direction, and smelling it, he looked up and said, "I believe it is a grouse, but it is not like ours." The next day he trotted before me like a turnspit, and became used to the ways of those parts; but I do not think we either of us very much cared for them. I am convinced from all I have seen—and I have watched dog-breaking very carefully since I was a boy of fifteen, both in Great Britain and Ireland, and abroad—that W. C. is right, and that you should break your dogs according to your game and your country. Your in-ground, your well-stocked moor, or partridge ground, will produce a more perfect machine; but it is your wild, not overstocked country, that forms the *beau ideal* of what the setter or pointer should be—speed, nose, pluck, and energy, combined with perfect stanchness, and that wonderful instinct or reasoning faculty which the dog possesses.

For developing these qualities I know no country like the Lews; and as I sit and look at *Whack*, and call back to memory our last evening on its hills together, poor Morris's old song haunts me. It runs, I believe,—

"And when the lesson strikes my head,
My weary heart grows cold."

CHAPTER V.

OUR FRED AND HIS HEAD NURSE.

AS I shall soon be taking leave of Aline and removing myself to Soval, it is only fit and proper that, before doing so, I should give some account of that distinguished firm, the joint tenants of the Aline shootings. They consisted of F. M., R. M., and myself.

I think there are few who know F. M. who will not allow (himself among the number) that Lucina, at his birth, turned into the goddess of good luck. I will give but one small instance of this, and then pass on. When a subaltern, quartered at Gibraltar, he kept a small yacht, in which he disported himself by sometimes going over to the Barbary coast to shoot wild boars or anything he could get. In one of these expeditions he was caught by a pleasant Mediterranean squall, which blew his sails, masts, and rigging anywhere, smashed his rudder, and carried his oars overboard, leaving himself and his boy sitting in his half-swamped

E

boat, like a she-bear with its cub. In this state he was tossed about the Mediterranean for two days, with nothing but a bottle of cherry-brandy for provision, when, fortunately, he was descried by Spanish smugglers. It was blowing still so hard that they could not take him on board, but flung him a rope, by which he managed to hold on, in imminent danger of being driven under water; and in this way he was towed into Malaga, whence he notified his safe arrival to the colonel of his regiment, thus accounting for his absence without leave. As nothing had been heard of him for a fortnight, his friends had been written to, and the untimely end of so promising a youth mourned over—the more bitterly as, at the very time of the announcement of his sad supposed death, a relation died and left him a very good property. So when our friend arrived at Gibraltar, he was consoled for the loss of his yacht by the intelligence of his accession of fortune, and at once got leave of absence to proceed to England and console his anxious relations. Thus, then, most assuredly Fred, as he was called, was not born to be drowned, and I never cared a straw for Loch Seaforth when he was on board; for if the little Spanish yacht and the craft (the *Heather Bell*) he had at Aline could not drown him, what on sea could? Besides, he was really a first-class boatman. I never saw one steer with an oar like him; and I verily believe that, once in particular, we should have been swamped while crossing from the Park to Aline after deer-stalking, with a very full boat, but for the manner he steered.

I have said before that our Fred was a very good sportsman, a good shot, a fine rider, and a capital fisherman. Of deer-stalking, however, he at that time had had very little experience; indeed, none of the party, myself excepted, knew much about deer, and my limited experience was confined to shooting in France and Germany, where stalking, as practised in the Highlands, is not known; though waiting and watching deer, particularly shooting them from trees near their favourite feeding-places, and also driving, are. I killed a great many fallow-deer in Ireland, and was suspected of having poached a great many stags when I lived at Gheramene, on the Upper Lake of Killarney; but, on the honour of a gentleman, I never did poach, or attempt to poach, a single one, though I might many.

Fred's first stalk was an important epoch in his life. M'Aulay took him to a stag, but the beast shifting a little during the stalk, he could not get nearer than some two hundred yards, and the only part of the stag he could then see to shoot at was not the entire head, but the angle formed by the jaw-bone with the head. M'Aulay said it was useless to shoot, and proposed letting the stag feed out of the spot; but Fred raised his rifle and shot him as dead as a stone, to Mac's wonderment—not to mine, for I am a believer in bottle-imps, and feel convinced that at that very moment Fred entered into compact with one, and that the day will arrive when the said imp will come and claim his reward. I have never doubted this, as I have often told him; and if there could be a doubt, his next stalk settled the question.

He got at a stag lying at the bottom of a steep glen, above which was some very high, rocky ground. All you could see of the stag, as he lay crouched down, was the top of the neck and shoulders—the back-bone, in short. The distance was over two hundred yards, and Fred shot him through the backbone, behind the shoulders, and he never stirred. After this the confidence between M'Aulay and F. M. was perfect; and the latter has often told me that whenever they get at a stag, he is as certain of him as if he was already gralloched. I have stalked a great deal with him, and I remember only one instance of his missing a stag,—and I have seen him make really marvellous shots, both standing and running.

He was, as I have already said, a very good game shot—not that Lews grouse required any very good shooting, as the birds never are too wild there. But he once killed a hundred brace of grouse to his own gun at Aline in one day, as already mentioned—a feat I would not have believed any man could have done; nor would he have done it, but for his imp. Few men I have ever seen could fish better; but here he had a failing—he was the most inveterate fish-poacher it was ever my fortune to encounter. When at Harrow, he and a confederate dragged every pond for miles round that sacred spot. He was never happy in the fishing way but when he was getting that blessed net of his into the water somehow or other. There was a nice little loch (Georgium) about four miles from Aline, good for sea-trout and an occasional salmon, but very sulky. We caught him one day coming home in his cart, with his net and some fish, having taken a haul in this our little sanctum, and looking as pleased as a schoolboy that had successfully pillaged an orchard. He could not resist poaching, even his own loch.

As to the womankind belonging to F. M., I do not at present feel myself up to describing them. Perhaps I may gain courage hereafter; let me content myself with saying now that they were of that sort that could safely be admitted into shooting quarters. I remember once an old gentleman who in days of yore filled his glens with his friends, and took immense pleasure in *giving away* all his quarters, was so particular about female influence, that he never allowed even his own wife to come into them.

There was, however, one particular female in F. M.'s establishment, that was so quaint in her ways, and such an endless source of amusement to us all, that I cannot withstand dedicating a few lines to her. This was one Celery, Fred's head nurse. In her vocation she was perfection. She doted on the children —they on her; and there was a conscious dignity about her which I never could make out—whether it proceeded from her idea of her importance as nurse to F. M.'s children, or the infinite privilege it was to the said children to be under the care of so sage a matron as herself. There was something in her not of the governess, but of the head of that wonderful establishment for the tuition of young ladies so graphically described in "Vanity Fair."

"Miss Halice," she would say to the eldest little totterer in the nursery, " you should consider the dignity and the importance of the position you hold as the eldest daughter of this house." "Miss Minnie," she would address the other little female, scarcely out of arms, " you should early learn to look up to Miss Halice for example and guidance." To both, as they toddled down stairs to dessert, " Young ladies, I hope you will not forget the manners you learn here, or do discredit to my nurturing."

But it was in her care of the boy of the establishment that the grandeur of Celery's ideas of the present and her mysterious predictions of the future were developed in all their full-blown beauty. To see her parade "Master 'Arry," as she called him, up and down Prince's Street! One morning, it being very cold, she had sensibly wrapped the little thing's head up in a woollen nightcap, and an inquisitive young lady insisted upon stopping her, and begging to see so fine a child. " No, mem; not to-day, if you please, mem. He is not got up as such a hinfant should be—he has not got his hat and feathers on." Another time, when he had his hat and feathers on, more anxious females accosted her, and insisted on knowing whose child he was, saying he looked like a little lord. Celery chuckled, pursed up her mouth, and answered mysteriously, "No, ma'am, he ain't a lord yet; but there is no knowing into what he may not turn—he might become a duke some day." Thus, you may see, Celery had ways of her own, and she expressed herself oddly. No doubt, her nursery education had been attended to, but her English had been neglected.

Mrs. Malaprop's confusion of the Queen's English and of ideas was not greater than Celery's; and these, added to the mystery of her communications, rather obscured the meaning of her quaint words. She was a very excellent woman, I believe, sincerely good and religious; and thought it right to keep a missionary box, into which she was always soliciting every one to put something. She was trying R. M. very hard one day, in vain; but at last she burst forth, "Now, dear Mr. M., do drop in something; there is no knowing where it is going to, or when it will come back to you." No one has yet been able to fathom the profundity of this speech.

But dear old Celery had yet other accomplishments, which must not be forgotten. In the frequent little festivities that used to take place at the birth or christening day of a little F. M., she was, of course, the mistress of the ceremonies. She brewed the best, and by far the strongest, toddy I ever drank in my life; and when, in the pauses of the pipers' strains, and after the Reel of Tulloch, perhaps she, by way of a little variation, on the earnest call of the company, sang the charming ditty, " Sweet Richmond 'Ill," one resigned oneself to one's fate, and, softened by her punch and beguiled by her melody, gave way to the spell, and Celery was the houri of the hour.

Years passed on, and one fine day, long after I had taken to Soval, I got a letter to say that C. was getting odd, and falling into a species of religious melancholy, and doing queer things. The only point on which there was no variation was her love and care for the missionary-box. I could make nothing of her, excepting that she had grown much more mysterious. She also was in a melancholy state about her young charges—her awful responsibility as to the future if the young ladies did not turn out so many young " Miss Frys;" if her young gentlemen were not fit and willing to carry her missionary-box cause throughout all heathendom. We began all to entertain the most serious fear that some fine morning, out of the sincerest love and anxiety for their spiritual welfare, and to secure the future salvation of her young charges, she might cut their throats and throw them into Loch Seaforth.

Pending these anxious fears, news came that rendered it necessary for both Fred and myself to go to England. It was all very well saying "go;" but how were we to go? It was winter, and during the winter time there was but one weekly steamer, and, unfortunately, just at this time this steamer was wrecked. A temporary one, it is true, was put on; but there was an interregnum of irregularity which put us both much out.

There was at that time a revenue cutter, a fine boat, commanded by a lieutenant in the navy, a very good officer and seaman, who had seen and done much good service. He is dead now, poor fellow! and, though *de mortuis nil nisi bonum*, still one may be allowed to allude to some of his peculiarities. He was a very neat-made, gentlemanlike-looking fellow, but not a giant, certainly; yet in no specimen of mortality I ever beheld did there exist such elements of noise. As if there was not din enough in the elements in those wild climes, he trained certain of his sailors to play upon some of the noisiest instruments, of all kinds, I ever heard: there was not one, but several, Bones. When in harbour, at Stornoway or elsewhere, he was perpetually scaling his guns. Then he never came ashore in his gig but accompanied by his band, and he was perpetually scaring the slumbers of the poor Stornowegians. A friend of mine was once inveigled into going on board the cutter to dine and sleep. He was nearly deafened by the band during the dinner and the evening; and all night, whenever there was the slightest chance of sleep, his host jumped into the cabin to know how he was getting on, or called out from his berth, with his speaking-trumpet, to inquire after the comfort of his bed. It is odd that, after this slight warning, my friend was rash enough to dine with him again, and induce me to do so, one Christmas Eve; and I do not think we shall either of us easily forget it. Of course the usual noises went on; but after dinner it came on to blow, as it can in those latitudes—so hard that, though we were in the harbour of Stornoway and not far from the shore, our skipper either would not or could not land us; at least, he said his boat could not get back, and he would not risk it. The gale was really frightful, and during the evening the mate came down to say we were dragging our anchors. There was no doubt of the fact. Chain cables and all sorts of things were to be let go and hauled upon all night, and I think that night was the origin of a deafness that has been a great discomfort to me since. But above the roaring of the wind, the creaking of cables and chains, and steam getting up and steam letting off, rose that little skipper's voice, and he outnoised everything. I was glad when morning came; and sure enough we had dragged, for we were all but on shore on the islands in the harbour.

This skipper had heard of the strait in which Fred and I were, and he sent us word that, if we would be in readiness, he would bring his cutter round into Loch Seaforth and take us all over the Minch to the mainland; and, in due course of time, in came the cutter and anchored opposite Aline—whether with the intention of really taking us away, I never could tell; but he said so, and he was a British seaman and a gentleman. The wind was awkward at all times for getting out of Loch Seaforth, and it would not do, as he said, for the week he passed there. And what a week! As for the band, it was always going, either on board or on shore. We were startled from our beds every morning with his guns to notify his readiness to sail, and by constant boats, always attended with part of the crew's band, to say he would not sail. Of course he always dined with us every day, and, though we were tired, stupefied—crushed, in short—his powers of noise seemed to increase in proportion to our prostration. At last, one night, he invented a new species of torture. He took two plates with rough borders, and rubbed and clattered them together, producing so excruciatingly painful and discordant an uproar—I can give it no other name—that some of our party rushed out of the room to preserve their senses. I think one day more would have sent us all to the nearest lunatic asylum, when, fortunately, the next morning—a bright, clear, frosty morning—a small steamer came into the loch, Fred having sent to Stornoway to beg the agent to send round the first steamer that turned up for us, and rescued us from our tormentor's grasp; and we steamed away most gladly, leaving him nothing but the high hills to awaken with his noises.

By-the-bye, it is worthy of remark that next summer, as we all steamed back again into Loch Seaforth joyfully, but a little subdued with two or three nights on board the steamer

—as we were all standing on deck and nearing joyfully our beloved Aline, all of a sudden I saw Fred's countenance change. "Bless that fellow! there he is again!" he remarked; and, true enough, there lay the cutter, *dressed*, as they say, with her flags and signals, and yards manned, welcoming our arrival with band, and salutes, and cheers, among which there was no mistaking the skipper's. It was, however, his last torment. He was on his way to Greenock to give up the command of the cutter, the term of his service being out. Well, peace be to his ashes; but I do not think anything so mischievously noisy could be at peace. If he went aloft, I think he must have destroyed the equilibrium of Heaven itself. If he went below, I think he must have tired out the devils themselves, who would have returned him to earth, not by their sovereign's commands out of jealousy for Madame Pluto, but from inability to bear him among them.

It was during this memorable epoch that poor Celery's malady reached its climax. When the little steamer hove in sight, everybody commenced doing the last things to the carpet-bags. Celery, making rapturous allusions to her responsibility, disappeared into the nursery, from which, in due time, she emerged with her charges, some of whom she delivered up to her subordinate; and then, seating herself at the end of the pier, on her own particular carpet-bag, of which she never for a second lost sight, with her little white terrier at her side, and holding "Master 'Arry" tight by the hand, she threw up her eyes to the bright blue sky above, and said, majestically, "My duties is performed, and you will find all is right; and now I resigns myself trustfully to a gracious Providence."

I always liked teasing her a little, and could not help saying I thought it would be fine to Portree, at any rate. She retorted rather spitefully, and practically enough, too, that "these frostes sometimes turned into bad weather," and she solemnly adjured me to go back into the house, and see if all was as it ought to be in her department. I could not help doing as she bade, and, going up to her nursery, found it arranged and in order as if her charges were coming in that night, not leaving it that morning. This struck us all as odd, and we kept our eye on her till we were all safely on board the little steamer.

We had a beautiful sail to Portree; there was not a ripple on the water; and one must have seen that country on a bright, clear, frosty day, when you could discern a midge almost on the top of Cliesham, to know how beautiful it can be. We slept at Portree, where a gentleman—or, at least, a well-dressed man—distinguished himself by a feat of chivalrous disregard of self I have seldom seen equalled. There were many passengers, and but scant accommodation at the hotel. The individual in question, then, on our landing, made the best use of his legs, and, arriving first, selected the largest and best room in the house, and secured his own possession, to the exclusion of all others, by locking the room up and putting the key in his pocket.

The next morning was as fine as the preceding, and we steamed on to Oban, where we arrived happily in the evening, and here poor Celery's mystery was solved. She had been more than usually careful of her charges, her white terrier, and particularly her carpet-bag. She had been more than ever awfully enigmatical in her views of the past and the future. We had all retired to our apartments, when sounds seem to issue from the sufferer's room. We all rushed to see what could the matter be. We opened the door, when lo! full-dressed and cross-legged like a Turk, sat Celery on her bed, the immortal carpet-bag by her side, her dog looking wistfully in her face; while his mistress, flourishing an empty whisky-bottle over her head, trolled out, not in the soft strains of "Sweet Richmond 'Ill," but in a deep, rich, almost bass voice:—

> "Old King Cole was a merry old soul,
>   And a merry old soul was he;
> He called for his pipe, he called for his bowl,
>   And he called for his fiddlers three."

Poor C.! from that time all was over with her. To the regret of all who knew that establishment, she had to go; but even in her fall, Celery was dignified, and she delivered over her missionary box, with all its contents, to her mistress, accounting for every farthing received, and begging her to remit the funds to their proper destination. So much of sympathy was felt by all for her misfortune—which turned out to be only that temporary giving way to whisky's charms that so often overtakes Southerners on their first acquaintance with the North—that she was very soon well placed again, and acquired, as she so well deserved it, the entire confidence of her new employers. I never heard of any whisky relapse, or another chant of "Old King Cole." In one thing, indeed, she showed her great good sense and good feeling.

F

She left off her missionary box, on the ground that "kimparisons was hodious." She still keeps up a close connection with F. M.'s family, and it is gala day when old Celery comes to pass a day with her "young charges," as she still persists in calling them.

CHAPTER VI.

OUR FIRM AND THE WHALES.

R. M. was also a first-rate sportsman at everything, and one of the very best men I ever saw in my life to face a rough country with a dog and get stuff out of it. He was, in his day, one of the best hill-walkers I ever knew; indeed, too good, for he was always walking at his dogs, his gillies, and any unfortunate man that went out shooting with him. He was a capital stalker, for he had the eye of a hawk and the bump of locality; but, being of a very excitable nature, he was not as cool as he might be when he came to shoot. He was always sighting and trying his rifle, and the white spots on the rocks and hills about were plastered with the lead of his trial bullets, showing the accuracy with which bull's-eyes could be made. Once, indeed, a memorable and most provoking instance occurred of this mania of sighting. They had been collecting sheep in Harris for the Falkirk fair, the Harris Hills not being then, as they are now, clear of sheep; and consequently the Aline Hills, Lewis, and Carneval, were full of deer, huddled together like driven sheep. To stalk them was out of the question, and therefore R. M. was placed in a pass while the forester and the gillies went round to manœuvre the deer to him. This they were doing well, while R. M. was amusing himself with surveying the prospect, and now and then sighting an innocent white lamb that was watching its mamma feeding. On came the deer, and they were all but within shot when our friend took a last sight at his pet lamb, forgetting that he had not uncocked his rifle; bang went both his barrels, bah-ah went the poor little innocent, pierced with both bullets, and back went the deer.

So amusing, and at the same time so thoroughly annoying, was the incident, that the Aline farming tenant, old Mr. Stewart, who had been a keen stalker in his day, never would hear of any payment for the lamb, saying that it was bad enough to lose such chances at the deer without having to pay for the lamb. The occurrence, however, had its annoyances. It got wind, and was, some years afterwards, the cause of considerable legal and uselessly ludicrous inquiry. A *red* (Lewisian for *chestnut*) horse was found dead in a peat-hole somewhere under Stachshal Hill, on the Soval ground. R. M. and I had been stalking there, and upon it found a good stag, which he unaccountably missed with both barrels. The dead horse being also found, as I said, in this locality, the lamb story was revived, and our friend, after he had left the island, got the credit of having potted the horse. Of course, the story grew into a good one, and I was one of the last to hear it; but when all but legal proceedings were about being instituted, I was enabled to say that I had watched the latter part of the stalk with my "prospect," the ground being too ticklish for more than the stalker; that I had seen both the stag and the red horse, who were in opposite directions; and that unless bullets, without a ricochet, flew backwards, neither of the two could have touched the horse. This sufficed for the legal question, but to this day the Lews gives R. M. the credit of missing the stag and killing the horse. However, notwithstanding all these little misadventures, few men would have beaten him as a stalker, for he was not to be tired or turned by difficulties; and as he grew older, and more up to his work, he became steadier, and was no mere poodle dog at his stalker's heel, as many of your fanaticos are.

Ah, me! the day—I remember it well—when we started early from Soval, and stalked away right past the Barvas Hills, on to near the Glen House on the Barvas Road, and round by Rosheval and the mouth of Glen Bhragair to my bothy at Diensten, killing a fine royal, whose head I am looking at now; and then, because we had left another stag somewhere near the glen's mouth, stalked the same ground the next day back again home, blank—a fine walk indeed, and we shall never do the like again. The home is gone, and more—all that made it then what it was! And poor *Bob*, as we called R. M., and I are now two old cripples, that can only live on the memory of those bygone happy days. But enough of this sad theme.

R. M. was a very good fisherman, and threw as long, as straight, and as light a line as anyone; but then he was always admiring his throwing, and casting too much line—the greatest mistake a man can ever make—more than he or anybody could ever command. There were few streams he could not cover. He had also a very pretty notion of dressing a good fly—a great qualification in a fisherman; not that

I am a believer in dressing flies by the riverside after the pattern on the water, at least for salmon or sea-trout fishing. Lastly, R. M. was a capital game shot, and therefore his dogs, when he had patience to give them time, were very good.

I suppose I must say something about myself, but it won't be much. The reader will, by this time, have found out that I am passionately fond of dogs, and not averse to sport of any kind; but, though shooting from childhood almost, not being early accustomed to good shooting, I never learnt to shoot. I was never quick, almost always most uncertain, and never could ascertain why, from youth till now, I remained decidedly a most indifferent shot, though I might be able to hit a haystack flying. I was and am passionately fond of fishing, and have killed a great number of fish in my life; but I never could throw—and never, I presume, shall be able to throw—a line as it ought to be thrown. I threw from the shoulder, not the wrist. I could kill a fish when I got hold of him—that I could do; and I never tired of fishing as long as fish were worth catching. The moment they get red and full of spawn, their heads big, and long snouts—bah! I don't care for them. I attempted dressing flies, and produced anomalous things—certainly not ephemera—though, strange to say, I once fastened a bundle of something on a hook that killed fifteen fish—kelts, mind you; but what won't they take? I did love stalking, indeed. I began well with a single rifle, was not the least excited, killed four out of five of the chances I had, and impertinently wondered how any living soul could miss a stag broadside on at, say, eighty to a hundred yards; and so, fired with ambition, I took to a double rifle—a wonderful weapon, made, at F. M's suggestion, by Askey, of Bedale—with which I broke so many bottles at long distance, that the said F. M. would stand no more. Had we had cups then at Aline I should have won them all. I made an example of cormorants and herons, even of gulls; but when it came to deer—oh! F. M.'s bottle imp sat across my sight, and no longer was my ear gratified with the dead thud of success, but grated by the ringing crash of some rock either over or under him. The fact was, I was afflicted with the stalking fever, and when I came to shoot I was like Gil Blas when, in the encounter between the robbers and Don Alvar and his suite, he shut his eyes and fired his carbine anywhere.

Such was our firm, and three good men and

true were we. We were all sitting together one of those fine days when there is nothing to be done but admire the prospect—if the midges will let you—with just mist enough on the hills to prevent stalking, no breeze for fishing, and grouse too small to shoot, when our notice was attracted by several boats appearing at the mouth of Loch Seaforth. Out went the *prospects*, and M'Aulay was summoned; after a long look through his glass, he remarked, shutting it up, with emphasis, and with that look of pleasure and determination which gleams in his eye when he sees a good royal:— "It's just the whalls." An electric shock seemed to pass through the whole party, and in less than no time every craft in the establishment was manned, and everybody seized every conceivable weapon of offence, and hurried into the boats. The whale boat, our own particular conveyance across Loch Seaforth, was manned by the best crew, under the special guidance of M'Aulay, who hoisted his flag on board of it, and then took command of the whole squadron, to watch the movements. The whales had been descried off West Tarbert Loch, in Harris, when all the inhabitants got into their boats, and, following them, "*put them,*" as it is termed, "*into Loch Seaforth.*"

The reader is not to imagine that the whales I am describing are the great whales. They are what are called the "bottle-noses," from twelve feet to twenty feet long, and they consort together and go in shoals—for what purpose I don't pretend to say, nor am I sufficiently read in natural history to say what their birth, parentage, or education may be. But they every now and then make a voyage of discovery to the Hebrides. When they come they produce great excitement, and their capture is a great object to the inhabitants, as each bottle-nose contains within itself a certain portion of very good oil. The method of capture adopted is, by following and flanking them at a very respectful distance, to get them into some sea loch, at the head of which lies some shoaling ground. An indented rock-bound loch is of no use. Having thus induced them to enter such a loch, you follow them up in the same manner, slowly and distantly, cautiously outflanking, but never pressing or disturbing them. Thus, as it were, left to themselves, they gradually advance up the loch, following their leader; and, if the tide and shoal and all be propitious, he will of his own accord take the shoal water, even sometimes beach himself on the sandy spit, when the whole band will follow him like a flock of sheep, and strand themselves. But, if you press them too hard, they will be apt to turn short round and make for sea again.

Now, Loch Seaforth is admirably adapted for a whale-hunt. The loch runs up from the Minch straight to Seaforth Island, about six or seven miles, pretty well iron-bound on both sides. At Seaforth Island, which is nearly opposite Aline, the lock turns almost at right angles, and runs by Aribhruich, where are some sharp rapids, up to Skipnaclet, its head. Here, or on the shoals above—the Aribhruich Narrows, as they are called—is the best place for stranding the bottle-noses. We, therefore, in our boat division, hugged the shore by Aline, so that, if they liked, they might take the sand and shingle between Aline and Harris, at the mouth of the Glenviedale river. Bottle-noses preferred passing up to Aribhruich, and seeing as much as they could before landing. When they had well passed, and when the other squadrons of boats hove within communicating distance, as soon as ever it was ascertained what squadron ours was, and that Murdoch M'Aulay was our skipper, the command of the whole fleet was by universal acclamation conferred on him.

The whales passed round the island without hesitation, and pursued their way upwards, our boats following slowly. There was little delay or stoppage till we came to the Narrows. There the whales paused, and did not much seem to relish the idea of putting their noses to the steam. We, of course, rested on our oars, awaiting their determination, and there we waited all night.

Towards dawn, as it was low water then, and it was quite clear that the whales were waiting for water, or something before proceeding higher—once past the Narrows, they were ours—and that could not come for some time, we, who had started shortly after our breakfasts without any luncheon, were getting hungry; so we rowed back to Aline to soothe our very clamorous stomachs, and, that done, returned without delay.

During our absence a reinforcement had joined our fleet, and a curious, and, as it turned out, a most unfortunate one it was. It was in the shape of one of the dirtiest, crankiest tubs of a boat, with the roundness, not the steadiness, of what was called at Westminster, in my day, "a punch-bowl," and as little hold in the water as a skiff. How it got round from Tarbert-in-Harris, whence it was said to come,

I cannot imagine. The crew consisted of three of the ugliest, noisiest, most ill-conditioned-looking viragoes of women I ever looked upon. No one knew, or, if they did know, would own them. There they were, perched up in their boat, like so many witches, barring their broomsticks. One of them sat upon a turf creel in the bows, knitting for her bare life. What Hebridean female, be she witch or not, does not, under every circumstance and every occupation, knit as if her bare life depended upon that exertion? Their voices set your teeth on edge, and their laughter made you try and stop your ears. It was evident they were bent on mischief, and that to maintain discipline with these three Gorgons was impossible; and so it turned out. The tide was now making fast. The rocks over which the rapids had been foaming were disappearing. We could see the leaders of the band of the bottle-noses moving about, and gradually feeling their way as to taking the Narrows. Half-an-hour's patience now, and our troubles would be repaid, and this band, like the last that had visited Loch Seaforth a few years before, would be ours; when, just at this critical moment, this triumvirate of demons, deaf to all entreaties, to offers of bribes innumerable, to threats (for it was proposed to fire across their bows to bring them to)—these demons, with an indescribable yell, broke loose, and being on the outside, but nearest, flank to the whales, rushed their boat at the Narrows with the incoming tide. Deep were our imprecations, for in a second the whales turned, and the game was up. I have seen a fox headed back into a small gorse in the middle of a fine grass country, with not a bush to shelter him for six miles, by a jealous tailor, and have, with a good many others, had feelings far beyond manslaughter; but I have often wondered since how those three female fiends escaped. Fortunately for them, however, so great was the confusion that followed their memorable exploit, that they got off unpunished, and were, I understand, never heard of more.

The moment the whales turned it was all over, unless they could be met and turned again at Seaforth Island. The whole fleet, with the exception of our boat, started at once for the island, with that object. Our admiral kept his position, and waited to see what the whales would really do, and, on their apparently remaining quiescent, we approached nearer. All at once he called out "Steady!" Ahead of us the loch seemed to seethe like boiling milk;

and, as again M'Aulay roared out, "They're coming!" and faced our boat hard at them, they came indeed, and for some seconds—I do not know how long—our boat stood on whales. We all looked at one another, and thought of those on shore; but it soon passed, and, to our infinite delight, we found our boat floating again. But it was touch and go. One crack of one whale's tail would have smashed our boat, and landing on the whales would not have been very pleasant. There was nothing to be done now but to join in the chase. We could not succeed in turning or making any hand of the band, and they made good their retreat to sea again. A good many shots were fired, and apparently a good many whales received rifle-bullets, which drew blood; but they sank, and I do not think that eventually more than three or four carcasses were recovered.

We all returned home, tired and disgusted; and we certainly did not lay our heads on our pillows with those feelings of Christian charity towards the three women that ought to fill the hearts of sinners.

CHAPTER VII.

SOVAL SHOOTING AND OLD TOM'S PEDIGREE.

IN 1853 I removed to Soval, where I remained till the Lews and I parted in 1869. I was monarch of all I surveyed, and my survey consisted, as far as my recollection goes, of some 75,000 acres, according to the Ordnance survey. A great deal of the ground was of little use for game, as there were several large villages or towns, as they are called, well populated, and a great number of minor hamlets. All along the west coast the towns came very thick, and in the immediate neighbourhood of those townships game could not be expected to abound. For several years I had no comrade, and I had my little principality, very like Robinson Crusoe, entirely to myself. By road, from Balallan Bridge to Sharbost, the extreme bounds of the shooting was over thirty miles—very grand, indeed; but how were you to get at the ground to shoot it? True, at that time there was very little indeed to shoot on the western parts; and towards Dalbeg and Sharbost one might travel miles without seeing a grouse, though there were woodcocks and snipes and plover. The first thing to do was to make out some abode from whence one could get at the larger portion of the ground, which from Soval was entirely impossible. How curious it is that in Scotland the lodge is always placed as far from the centre of the ground as possible!

At that time there was no inn, as there now is, at Garrynahine; therefore I was constrained to build myself a bothy, kennel, and stable on the top of Diensten Hill, about seven miles from Soval, whence I could get at the heart of the shooting, and which was about three miles and a half from the best river; and in this said bothy I located a keeper. In the neighbourhood of Diensten, too, were to be found the few deer that were then on the ground; for at that time the only part of the Lews that was forested was Kenraisort, and there were deer going over parts of the Soval ground at particular seasons, passing from south to north, and *vice versâ;* and the stags obtained were good. I therefore never killed the hinds, but let them increase, in hopes of attracting the travelling stags, which succeeded very well till the foresting Aline and Harris so diminished their migration that it all but ceased. Diensten Hill—where, as I said, I built my bothy—commanded one of the finest, if not the finest, view in the country. The whole line of Park, Lewis, and Harris, and the Uig Hills, lay like a panorama before it, and of a fine day it was truly such a view as was seldom looked at; but it had its disadvantages. This same hill, when it was not fine—which it is not always in the Hebrides—was about the windiest spot in that very windy country. Diensten bothy did not originally cost a great deal, but its repairs did. In roofs and windows I hardly know what it did not cost. They were perpetually blowing off or in. On one particular occasion I had just considerably enlarged the bothy, and newly thatched it from end to end; when, as we were all located there for the opening of the grouse campaign in the Diensten district, it began to blow a little after daybreak. My then keeper, John Munro, came to me, advising the party to get up, as he thought the bothy was going. The thatch certainly was, and he had been three times blown off the top of the bothy into his garden trying to secure it. I got up to see what was going on, as the others were too lazy; and lo! there was the roof making its way, by instalments, fast back through the air to the place whence it came, the side of a well-heathered hill. (N.B. Our roof was of heather). We breakfasted early that morning *al fresco*.

From Diensten it was about eleven or twelve miles across the muir to Dalbeg, where lived a great ally of mine, the then ground officer, an excellent man, John M'Kenzie, who was of much assistance to me in grouse preservation, and who had a comfortable slate-roofed house, where I used to locate for a week or a fortnight at a time for shooting purposes, and where also I built a kennel.

Having thus rendered it possible to get at my ground, I then turned my mind to see what was to be done with it as far as grouse were concerned. The prospect was not promising, for the stock of birds, from the causes already given, was, for the extent of ground, miserably small. On large tracts there were actually none, and the first time I shot from Callernish Inn to Dalbeg, some eight miles across the muir, my grouse-bag consisted of one old cock. Fortunately we had three or four very good breeding seasons, one after another. A great deal of the ground consisted of flats and glens, surrounded with hills. I do not think there ever was more beautiful hunting country formed for the different varieties of winged vermin and other enemies to grouse, that abounded; and, but for the great number of peat bogs and peat mosses, which were a great protection, I think birds never could have held their ground. In my opinion, Highlanders—certainly Hebrideans—are not the best trappers in the world; they have not system enough for the work, and are not early trained up to it. I once remarked to a Hebridean keeper the number of hawks I had seen on such and such ground, and recommended attention to it, when he silenced me by saying that "hawks did not pay for shoeleather." An eagle is worth money to stuff; an otter's skin fetches a good price, and this accounts much for the keenness after them. There is also one thing to be said about trapping in those parts. There are no trees on which to set traps, and wood is a scarce article. They can then only be set on cairns or piles of either stones or peats, which attract the attention of the natives to a certainty, and the traps stand a very poor chance. But somehow we managed, at their breeding time, by degrees to get rid of a great many hawks, ravens, and crows. I decidedly objected to the destruction of eagles; for who does not like, even at the cost of several grouse, to see an eagle soar? Besides, I don't believe they do such a great deal of harm; I will back the gulls against them any day. Against those birds I declared war to the knife. There was a beautiful freshwater loch, Trialaval by name, in the centre of the shooting, shaped something like a star, with numerous bays and outlets, or rather inlets, for burns. It was some three or four miles long, but how many round I never could make out, for it was almost impossible to get round it, unless one knew the particular fords to cross the different streams that ran into it. On this loch were several islands, on which nested every species of gull that can possibly be imagined. It was really an extraordinary sight to go up there at the time the young gulls were coming out, and watch them taking their first lessons in the air and on the water, and getting ready for their migration to the sea, some three or four miles off.

Well, I settled the whole community by year after year systematically destroying their eggs, till, as Paddy said, "I made them lave that" so completely that they disappeared; and I know that as they became scarcer the grouse increased considerably.

Having thus taken measures, as far as practicable, against the increase of vermin, I proceeded, as far as I could, to divide all the ground into separate beats, never shooting the same ground over twice for grouse. For some seasons, as far as I could possibly manage it, I never shot hens, but killed every old cock I could get at, in season or out of season, on the ground; poached him, in short, anyhow I could. I shot the broods always lightly, and thus, by degrees, spread the birds out over the whole ground, so that parts of the north ground, where there was really nothing at first, became as good as the south; but the process was very slow indeed, and it entailed great labour. To shoot the ground in this way, we had often—besides driving some six or seven miles along the road, where we left our trap to return in—to walk three, four, five, or six miles to our beat, shoot that beat, and then walk the same distance back across the muir to our road or our bothy. Few men could do this, or would do it if they could; and therefore, though I should have been glad of a companion, the sort I wanted was hard to find.

I said above that I never went over the same ground twice for grouse; but, in the woodcock season I again went over much of the ground, particularly the glens, and then I never spared an old cock. Thus I gradually cleared the ground of that worst of all vermin.

There were two great difficulties to contend with in getting up game in the Lews—viz., egg-stealing and heather-burning. And first as to egg-stealing. In the spring of the year, just about the breeding season, it is the custom for the women and children—the men being occupied at the different fishing stations—to go out to the shealings, as they are called, with their cattle. These shealings are temporary turf cabins, scattered all over that part of the muir allotted for grazing to the different townships, or towns, which extend over a large portion of the shooting. It is necessary that this should be done, as otherwise all those parts of the muir near the towns which should be reserved for autumn and winter feeding, would be grazed off early, and the remoter parts left untouched. Now, conceive a whole population of women and children let loose over your ground in the nesting and hatching season! The consequence is, that a general search is made for the nests, which sharp eyes soon find. When found, the nest is watched till pretty full of eggs, when a snare is set for the hen, who is soon caught and eaten, and then the eggs are taken. Against this system no amount of keepering can avail. The wholesale destruction that takes place may be conceived. In some places it amounts almost to annihilation, and accounts in some measure for the number of single cocks seen about. If even any egg-stealers be caught, the difficulty of punishing the culprits is great; and so is the expense, for the canny Scot wisely introduces a clause into your lease that the expenses of the prosecution are to be borne by the renter of the shooting, though he can only prosecute through the Fiscal, whose duty it is, *ex officio*, to perform that office. I, therefore, always eschewed prosecutions; and, at last, by being well known to the general population over my shooting, having been the means of doing them some little service, having popular keepers who well knew the habits of the people, and by a little bribery of so much per brace to the herd of every shealing, I was able, in some degree, to stop the wholesale destruction that sometimes takes place. But still, the system of shealing —which cannot be prevented, though it might be very much modified—is a bar to that steady increase of grouse that good preservation might otherwise produce.

Now, as to the other difficulty, of heather-burning, there was too much and too little burnt. The sheep-farmer, who paid high rents —as he said, at least,—not being bound by his lease to burn only a certain portion of the ground yearly, and that only as sanctioned by the keepers, of course practically burnt as he liked. It was all very well recommending him from head-quarters not to burn but as agreed upon between him and the shooting tenant; but self-interest is self-interest; and, though I generally pulled well with the sheep-farmers, still, very often, just what ought not to have been burnt was burnt. Now, as to the poor tenants' grounds, it was precisely the reverse. They did not care much about burning, but, as to the rank old heather that ought to have been burnt, I never could get them to burn that, because they declared it was the only protection they had for their sheep in winter; and it would have been as wrong as it would have been impolitic in me to have used anything like coercion with them. Between the two systems, however, we throve badly. Over large tracts we had either no heather or too much.

My factotum at this time was one Cameron, who had been Burnaby's henchman, and was a jack-of-all-trades, and at that time a considerable favourite. He was a mainland man, somewhere from Lochiel's country, and I christened him "Lochiel." He was a very clever fellow, and could do anything he liked. He was a good walker, and knew a good deal more about shooting than he cared to let you know. He pretended never to have handled a gun, but he could shoot very well. He had a good eye for a deer, though he always professed "being no acquaint with them." He was the second best fisherman I ever saw in my life. My old Davie at Killarney was the best; but then I don't think Cameron ever let any one know how well he could fish, or how long a line he could throw. He was a very good boatman, and held a boat for fishing—a very great art—better than any-one I have ever fished with, except the aforesaid old Davie. He was a very good carpenter, and decidedly handy at anything. He was fond of his pony and his dogs, and took good care of them. But then he had a fault, and it was a strange one. It was not whisky, it was not temper; but he passed his whole life thinking and contriving how he could save himself trouble and avoid doing any particular thing that he knew must be done. He was a lazy man, of great energy if he liked. Sandie, too, came into my service about this time, as a watcher in the far west side at Dalbeg; but it is not the time to speak of him yet.

My dog-team was not at this time what it afterwards became; I was only getting my kennel up. True I had Old Tom, a host in himself, then young, and his little son Jock, the offspring of his youth; Grouse, the first, a beautiful black and tan setter, that I bought of Burnaby, and as good as gold; a wild demon of a black, white, and tan setter bitch; Lady, a very good black and tan setter bitch, given me by poor Douglas of Scatwell, who had a nice kennel of beautiful Gordons; and Dick, a great big handsome liver and white setter, very useful in his way. His nose was wonderful, and I always took him out with little Jock. Dick telegraphed grouse at extraordinary distances, when Jock bulleted in for a quarter of a mile and took you to the birds. Between them they were very effective. But, before concluding this account of my dog-team, I must say a word or two about my dear Old Tom and his pedigree.

Fifty-four years ago, when at Cambridge, I purchased, on the recommendation of a Yorkshire friend, a very thoroughbred-looking, handsome, and excellent pointer-dog, called Clinker, whose breed, derived from that of the celebrated Colonel Thornton, had been in my friend's family many years. This dog died a few months afterwards of dysentery; but the terms of his purchase having been that I was to have a bitch puppy of the same breed, in the spring of 1818 a beautiful little one arrived at my rooms, and commenced our long acquaintance by tearing an Herodotus to pieces. *Die* (so we called her) was a most precocious animal, played all sorts of tricks, was lost, cried, found, and then, spite of all college authorities, domesticated as the faithful companion of my every hour. Beautiful, faithful, sagacious, perfect in the field, Die was allowed to be the handsomest and best pointer in the University and its vicinity. There may be some persons living still who remember her and her picture (as painted by one whose real vocation certainly was animal painting). I refused for her what then were fabulous prices; but no gold would have tempted me to sell poor Die, whom, on my going abroad, I gave to my dear friend, her painter, who loved and valued her equally with myself. With him she passed the remainder of her days, well known both in Staffordshire and Cheshire; and from a daughter of hers, very like herself and called after her, I bred a litter of puppies by my black-and-tan pointer, Fowler (from his performances called the *Professor* by those who may yet remember him in Ireland and in Norfolk).

And here comes a singular link in the pedigree. Shortly after littering young Die took the distemper, and, being obliged to leave home, I left her and her litter in charge of my cousin's huntsman, who falsely reported her and her young dead. One had survived, which he sold to a neighbour. Of this neighbour I some years afterwards purchased Whack, one of the best (if not the best) muir dogs I ever owned, and, after many pressing inquiries as to his parentage, it came out that his dam was my purloined puppy, his sire a fox-hound. This accounted to me for a something in Whack that was constantly reminding me of poor old Die. I crossed Whack with Meg, an excellent and fine bitch from the Rokeby kennels. Meg was a cross of Lord Wharncliffe's and Lord Althorp's (the Minister) breeds, supposed to be the two best of their day. From Meg, before I got her, sprang many of the Rokeby pointers, which were, when I knew them, among the handsomest and best I ever saw, and I understand their character is still the same. From Whack and Meg came Venus, or Vin, a small but very strong bitch, who was as good as anything could be. Untiring, she was gifted with great nose, sense, and sagacity. Vin never bred till she was nine years old, when she produced, by Nathan (a sire dog of Mr. Edge's, given by that gentleman to the late Hon. Henry Howard, as a fine specimen of his breed), the subject of this long story, Tom, or Old Tom, as he is generally called.

It is possible that there are still living some two or three sportsmen who knew Tom, and when I say he did all but talk to us out shooting, they would vouch for the truth of my statement.

I once sent him out with a friend staying with me, accustomed to dogs, and on his return he said :—

"I have not only had a good day's shooting, but the most agreeable and extraordinary companion I ever shot with: Tom has been talking to me all day, and telling me where he was going, and where I ought to go."

This was perfectly true, for it is his habit. Every man has, of course, the best dog in the world, though I do not pretend to say Tom was; indeed, I have had better myself, but never saw one of his sagacity.

Lews is a hard country for dogs to find game in—hilly, with hillocks; so that you cannot keep your dogs in sight, or they you. When Tom finds anything and does not see me, he is not fool enough to stay there for ever; he comes and looks for me, and when I see him, knowing what he means, I walk to him, when he takes me up to his game. But I have had other dogs do this, though not to the same extent. This, however, which I am going to relate, I never have seen.

Tom backed as well as a dog could; but if I was not in sight when the dog he was backing stood, Tom came to look for me, and having found me, brought me up to him; and his manner of introducing me to the dog, or the dog to me, might suggest a sketch to Landseer.

I hunted poor Tom thirteen seasons, and could never tire him; and if the fastest of my black-and-tan setters (and I had some very fast) was out, Tom would always take and keep the outside range. He was also an excellent and sagacious retriever—pointers, *par parenthèse*, always making the best when properly trained. In the coldest of days he would retrieve bird after bird out of the numerous lochs round which most of our shooting lay. I once winged a grouse, which ran towards a burn, and as Tom was retrieving it, I tailored another in the same fashion, who also made for the same burn. Tom stopped, and looked me hard in the face: he was singularly tender-mouthed, and the bird was alive in his mouth; so he shifted him gently till he came to his neck, which he squeezed sufficiently to stop any more running, and then quickly retrieved the other. I could go on, with the garrulity of my years, about my old dog for ever; but I must hasten the burthen of my story and conclude.

For Tom's pedigree I can only give the assurance of a gentleman's word. At a dog-show no one would have looked at him, for he was not a large "upstanding" dog, as the term is in these days, when dogs are judged by size and weight, as if they were to be eaten; yet he was probably as highly bred as any pointer in Great Britain, without the disadvantage of any in-and-in breeding. I would not exchange his blood for any in the kingdom, though I have always wished to cross it with some other as good, and as sagacious. You may increase this rare quality of sagacity by proper breeding to a great extent; you have then only to take care (but how much care!) not to hinder its development by what is called *breaking*.

Such was the shooting at Soval when I commenced. In my next I shall describe the fishing.

CHAPTER VIII.

SOVAL FISHING AND ARTIFICIAL SPATES.

THERE were two rivers attached to the Soval shooting at the time I took it—the Laxay, distant about three miles and a half; the Blackwater, about ten from Soval, three miles and a half from Diensten bothy. And first we will speak of the most distant river. There are two branches of the Blackwater—one running from a loch that I called New Loch, another running from another loch, called by me Loch Dismal.

About these two lochs the fish ran up by other smaller burns and lochs, but we never thought of fishing beyond these lochs. The two arms of the river joined together between Diensten and Garrynahine, and then the river becomes the Blackwater. From the junction there are two or three miles of rough water before you come to the first legitimate salmon pool. I call it *legitimate;* for, though I have done such a thing as catch a fish in the rough water above this pool, yet, generally speaking, fish don't stay in it, but run through for the two lochs. From this *legitimate* pool to the Major's pool, about a mile, when there was plenty of water and you knew it well, the fishing, to my mind, was always charming; for the gentlemen were very merry, and dodged about in the little narrows and pools in a very artful way. I first discovered the charms of this part of the water, for even Burnaby had never killed a fish there till I found it out, and never used to think of beginning to fish till he reached the Major's pool. From this pool to the big pool was about another mile and a half of charmingly varied water—pools, streams, and narrows; but it required fishing, though not long casting. It used to be "nuts" to me, sniggling a fish out of a corner that no man "unacquaint," as we say, with the water would dream of trying. The big pool, and the stream running into it, was the crack cast of the river; but I confess it was not my pet, for when in prime order it was necessary to cast a long line in the teeth of the wind, or rather across the wind, three-quarters against you, so that it was all but impossible to prevent your line bellying; and your fish rose on a curved, not a straight, line, which is not as it should be. I have often wondered one kept one's eyes in those gusty days, when you not unfrequently got your fly back smart in your face. But what with the wind and the stream, when you hooked a fish there, he fought. Strange to stay, though the pool was alive with fish, and rising in all parts by the weeds, you seldom took one anywhere but in the stream and its entrance into the pool between the two high banks of sedges. If by chance you ever did rise a fish in other parts, he generally beat you, and got off.

I put a little boat on this big pool, and got very nearly drowned two or three times, but never did anything to repay me for the trouble. From the big pool there was about half a mile of still, deep water, with little or no stream, but full of fish. When the wind was right—anything east, north, or south-east was useless, as it was still water on all the good casts—there were plenty of fish to be got, and here generally lay the heaviest fish. From the end of this long still water there was about a mile or so of rough water, in which you occasionally got sea-trout, and I have caught grilse. You then came to the pools into which the tide ran up near the Garrynahine Inn and bridge. There occasionally, particularly in the latter end of the season, you got fish; and if you

watched the turn of tide well, and caught the
pools as the fish were coming in, and before the
tide had made too much, you might get a good
many sea-trout. I once got eighty-seven, but
they were small. From this description it will
be seen that the Blackwater was a very nice
little river. It was no fine Highland or Irish
stream, but it had plenty of fish; and it had
one thing about it I never saw equalled—it was
the best rising river I ever threw line on. If
you treated it properly, and there was wind,
you would always kill fish, for there was a good
deal of deep water and pools; and when the
streams and pools would not fish for want of
water, the still, deep water always would when
there was wind—and it is not often the Lews
is without *that*. Many a happy hour have I
passed on its banks, and many a fish have I laid
on them; and, to my mind, they took the charm
of the Soval ground from it when they deprived
it of the Blackwater, and the sooner they unite
the two again the better. I and my comrade,
T. D., had probably better sport there when we
fished than any others are likely to have again.
I do not say this as boasting of our prowess,
for we were no better than our neighbours—
certainly I was not. But I loved the dear
stream so well that I always treated her as I

would my lady-love. I wooed her gently and considerately, and never asked of her too much. I never frightened her with vulgar, glaring, overgrown buzzards or colours, or ruffled her fair surface with strong cables, or shook great glaring poles about her smiling face. Our rods were wands, our tackle the gossamer's web, our flies scarce more than midges; and then, pleased and enchanted with our entertainment, left her to her soft repose, and never bored her with too much attention, or called too soon to inquire about her.

Believe me, there is no such mistake made in fishing, if you want a river to remain good, as working at it every day. It does not answer in a large river even, still less in a small one, where every fly you cast in the water is seen by every fish in it. I never fished the Blackwater two days running, except in very heavy water. It would be better to give it two days' rest for one of work, and in low water, and when not fishing weather, to leave it alone altogether. You may catch a fish; but how many do you scare? Heaven defend me from one of your very keen fishermen, who rushes at a river in all weathers. I have as great a horror of him as ever old Noll had of Sir Harry Vane. Why is it that a *terra incognita* in fishing at first produces such good sport? Simply because the fish, poor innocents, don't know the difference between a natural and artificial fly, or what a fly is. But they soon learn it. Flogging a river for ever, because you *may* catch a fish, is like disturbing good shooting ground on a bad day, when you thrash yourself, your dogs, and your men, all to no purpose, make yourself exceedingly uncomfortable, spoil the beat, and, if you do get anything, it is scarce worth bringing home. There is a certain amount of folly in being over keen. If you must have exercise, go out and get yourself as wet as a shag; but why drag everyone else into discomfort?

I said that there were two branches of the Blackwater, one issuing out of the New Loch, the other out of Loch Dismal. The branch out of New Loch was far inferior, to all appearance, to that from Loch Dismal, yet it was possible to kill fish in the one, but not in the other. There was some long, deep, sludgy water that you could jump over, and one or two little pools, which in flood water held fish, and rising fish too. It was my great delight, when my comrades were on the river, to betake myself to these quaint little places, and many a fish I got out of them. In the narrows it was great fun. You hooked a springy little gentleman, who jumped on the opposite bank. If you were by yourself, and could not clear the river, you had nothing for it but to pull your fish back into the water, fight him there, and bring him out on your own side, if you could. Or, perhaps, when hooked, Salmo rushed up one of these narrows, and in following him you were brought up by a cross ditch, filled to the bank with the overflow, and you had to stand snubbing and turning him, which, with light tackle and small flies, is not always so easily done. In the other branch of the Blackwater I remember killing but one grilse, and that in a small pool, or rather hole, where we hunted him about, and caught him with a landing net. Both Loch Dismal and New Loch held fish, particularly towards the end of the season; but I never found the salmon there, or in any loch save the Gremsta Loch and Loch Valtos, rise well to a fly. I believe the country people kill a good many with a worm, and when the water is deep enough they will run at a minnow. But, though there can be no doubt that spinning a minnow as it should be spun, and fishing a worm well under water, as Tom Stoddard does at Kelso, are very high angling accomplishments, perhaps higher than throwing a fly, I don't care for killing a fish—I mean a salmon—with aught but a fly.

Such is the Blackwater in its state of nature, which it was not when first I went to Soval, or rather the year after. The bag-nets—those charming engines, invented, I believe, for the destruction of rivers—had been taken off, only to be replaced after the angling was let, and in the very spot where they should not have been. I thought, by my lease, to have guarded against their being so placed; but a Scotch lease is a queer instrument, even of law, and the Ordnance map, which one would have supposed to have been conclusive evidence of locality, was not so considered. So there they were, and I had nothing to do but grin and bear it. Now, at even the mouths of great salmon rivers, bag-nets are bad enough, but when the rivers are not large, and very shallow, if the season is dry the fish cannot get up. They try, poor things, but in vain, and have nothing to do but with each retiring tide to drop back into the jaws of the ever-open bag-net. I had to go through this pleasant pass, till really the fishing got so worthless that I had serious thoughts of letting Clarke, the then lessee of the Gremsta angling, have it; for the fish could not get up, generally speaking, till late on in the season, and then I, for my part, don't much care for killing them.

When Salmo has the smallest of heads buried in his shoulders, with the most delicate mouth, and, like a little fat pig, is as broad as he is long, and as white as silver—good. But reverse the picture, and let him have a long head, with a big, bony mouth, as tough as leather, and a red, ugly, shiny-looking body—*a Dios, señor*, he is not my fish. He is little sport to kill, and—I own to being a *gourmet*, not a *gourmand*, in fishing—not nice to eat. In this state, then, memory, not inspiration, came to my aid. I bethought me of the Costello, in Galway, by whose pleasant side I had, in former days, killed buckets-full of fish; and, in imitation of what I had there seen practised, I dammed up Loch Dismal. Across the mouth of this loch I erected a dam and sluice similar to the common mill-dams of the country, taking care, of course, not to shut the sluices so close as to run the branch of the river dry. I thus kept back water enough to create an artificial spate, which I let go exactly in time to meet the high spring tides that bring the fish up to the rivers' mouths, which they take, wind and water permitting.

I found the experiment answer perfectly,

and over and over again I ascertained to demonstration that the fish took the river with my artificial, just as they would with a natural, spate. By judiciously keeping up a supply of water, I freshened up my river as it grew low, and brought up, ever and anon, fresh fish. I also, by the same process, sent to sea early the foul fish, which I had previously known remain in the river till the middle of July; thus rendering a double service—making the foul fish go to sea, and, consequently, return from it earlier, and preserving the fry from the wholesale slaughter made on them by their unnatural and voracious parents while waiting in the pools for water to get down. My belief is, that but for this plan the fish would have suffered much more than they did from the bag-nets, from whose maw I thus rescued not a few of my finny friends. This, however, I did not do without exciting the dire wrath of the bag-net men. To be sure, it was tantalizing to see the beautiful shoal they had calculated on daily diminishing with their abominable engine, on its return with each retreating tide from the fruitless attempt to take the river, whisked up at once by so singular a stream.

At first it was called an illegal act, an interference with vested rights; but that soon fell to the ground, as the river, from source to sea, lochs and all, belonged to me. The dam is six miles from the sea, and there is no trap or net of any sort to catch the fish, for may this hand wither if ever it assails the noble *Salmo salar* with a heavier weapon than an honest, well-dressed, light-cast fly! And so they had but to grin and bear it. And so then they changed the burden of their song. They condoled with my ignorance; they besought me, for my own sake, not to ruin my river, to spoil my own sport. Poor dear, considerate souls! And they adduced a wonderful proof of the mischief I was doing myself; which, by the way, got into print. A particular spate they said I had sent down had stirred up all the black mud in the river, sent it right in the teeth of a shoal of fish taking the river, and driven the fastidious creatures back to sea, where 300 of them were taken in the nets that night; as if a natural spate never stirred up mud at all!

A charming story—pity it was not true; for, unfortunately, that year being the last of the bag-net lease, and not wishing any disputes, I had never put my sluices in operation. They were safely housed in my stable! But some very ingenious workmen employed to gas-tar a bridge over the river, just where the salt joins the fresh water, chose the period of the high spring tides to do so; and, not content with botching their work, and dropping a good deal of tar into the river, to save themselves the trouble of removing the remains of the gas-tar cask, emptied it into the river, which, thus fouled, the fish would not take. I passed the bridge just after the performance of this notable exploit, and angry enough I was, though not the least astonished at the result. I thus saved my own angling; but did more good than this, for the Gremsta also profited. I am not one of those who imagine that so good a food as salmon is to be kept merely for anglers' amusement; but I do say that small rivers and small estuaries cannot stand close fishing—that in remote districts like the Hebrides, where there is no nearer market than Glasgow, and where the communication then was not so good as it is now, the netting-rent was not very remunerative to either lessor or lessee, and to expect to continue both netting and angling-rent could only end in grief to both. When netting is carried on closely, the almost invariable consequence, too, is that the size of the fish diminishes much. Before I put my sluices in operation I hardly ever got anything but dabs of fish, and the average of weight was small; but after they had been working for some years, the average very much rose, and they increased not only in quantity but in weight. Just as the river became a good one, however, it was severed from the shooting—a great mistake, in my opinion, for it very much added to the charm of Soval; and I think that eventually the wisdom of reuniting the two will be seen.

The other river in the Soval shooting was the Laxay, or Lakassay. It was about three miles and a half from Soval Lodge, and ran a course of some five miles, from Loch Trialaval to Loch Valtos. It was a shallow river, with not above three or four pools in it, and those very sheltered; and, except on odd days, the fish were sulky. Loch Valtos was a nice loch, and very good for sea-trout. There was, then, a mile more river from Valtos to the sea, or rather tideway, with two or three good casts for salmon; but they generally held sulky fish. At the time I first went to Soval salmon did not abound in the Laxay, and no wonder, for it was close fished with net and cable, and also foul-fished—a net being sunk across the mouth of the river, and kept there, so that it was all but impossible for fish to get up. It had also been well cruived. Fortunately, I caught them at their foul fishing, cut their net to pieces, and watched them so close, that they made a sort of compromise, and I got rid of the nets for a *con*sideration, as the Highlanders pronounce the word. The river, however, was so shallow, that, though I caught a great many sea-trout, I got very few fish. At last, seeing the success of the patent floods at the Blackwater, I tried them on the Laxay, and, to a certain extent, succeeded very well, for I caught one day more fish in the Rock and Reedy pools—the two good pools between Trialaval and Valtos—than I had ever caught in the whole river all the previous years of my tenancy. But it was up-hill work making sluices there. I tried in three or four different places, but not very successfully; for, though the river was very shallow, Loch Trialaval was a large body of water, and two or three times my sluice and embankment disappeared, and it required both care and expense to make them stand, and sometimes there were great floodings and overflows. Once I nearly drowned half the township of Laxay when out at their shealings; but they were quiet folk, and we were good friends, and I made them fords and put out stepping-stones, and, fortunately, there was no necessity for any coroner's inquests. They did say I drowned one old woman, cart and all; but, fortunately for me, as I was able to prove that the poor creature came to her untimely end ten miles from my scene of action, on the high road to Stornoway, by her cart going off the road into a burn in a state of flood and falling on her, I escaped all suspicion, even of womanslaughter, better than R. M. did the red horse misdemeanour. If I did not make the river what I wanted, I succeeded well with Loch Valtos, for it held a great many fish; and when I first arrived they rose well, and we used to have some very good sport in it. But one thing I never could account for. As the salmon increased the sea-trout decreased, and from being a very good loch for them, it became most indifferent; they decreased both in quality and size. Can any of the wise account for this?

There were very large fish in the Laxay, and it was a very early river; but I never got a dozen spring fish in it during the years I held it. I believe the fish began running in December and stopped in March, or before, just as they used to do in Killarney; nor did I ever, except in one or two instances, get in it very large fish, though I have killed kelts in spring that must have been 25 lb. or 30 lb. weight, and a great many of them. But the Laxay fish were, I think, larger than the Blackwater fish, and they certainly were a great deal better.

Besides these two rivers, there were at the west side smaller rivers and lochs—the Carlowy loch and river, and part of the Bhragair and Sharbost rivers, which no doubt held fish; for off Carlowy Head was a good netting station. They were not, however, worth much for angling; at least, though I often tried, I never did much in them. I have caught a sea-trout and a salmon or two; but they are not rising rivers. A non-rising river, of which I have seen many, is to my mind useless for angling purposes, and you had best consign it to the nets. There were also dotted all over the shooting fresh-water lochs innumerable, in which were good store of brownies. I never could get them to rise as they should to trout-flies, used in fair angling fashion, though they would rise to ottering; but one doesn't lose one's time on a good day at *that*, with salmon to kill. Moreover, they were the worst brownies to eat I ever tried.

Thus, I think I have shown that Soval as it was had within its boundaries great attraction for a wild, amphibious animal like myself, half otter, half colley, never happy but when dabbling about something, weather permitting—very fond of his dogs, and delighted in exploring lochs in little cobles, of which I had a fleet, and with no one to interfere with me. Let me now conclude this long yarn with a bit of practical advice to the large community of letters and renters of shootings and fishings.

There is a custom prevalent in some parts of Scotland better honoured in the breach than in the observance. I allude to the custom of some proprietors reserving in their lettings of rivers a right of sending—sometimes one day in the week, sometimes oftener — their own friends to fish on rivers so let. Now, I do not think a more unwise or, without the slightest wish to use hard terms, a more unfair thing can be done. You say it is one of the conditions of the letting; but, let me ask, when you let a shooting, do you retain a right to send your friends to shoot over the ground you let? or would any one in his senses take a moor or a forest on such terms? Why, then, am I to be expected to pay a high rate for a river, preserve it well, and, on the few salmon-fishing days the year brings round, run the risk of finding the proprietor's friends fishing my pet pool? It is asking too much of poor human nature to stand this. No one more enjoys walking by the side of any one fishing, if he can fish, showing him honestly the good casts and how to fish them, landing his fish, doing everything, in short, for him, except giving him my own particular pet fly—than I do. I can do it for days together. But loafers, or the proprietor's friends, coming as a matter of right—few or far between as may be—is another thing. There is pride and pleasure in the one, the devil and all his imps in the other. No proprietor should ever ask, no lessee ever consent to, such a condition. I go further still. No clean-bred gentleman should ever take advantage of such a privilege, and fish another man's water at that man's expense. I would not, and our friend Fred, I know, would not do it.

There is yet another point. This reservation contains within itself the fruitful germ of misunderstandings, heart-burnings, and all manner of strife and discord. I have known it work most unpleasantly, and become the *fons et origo malorum* that otherwise would never have arisen.

CHAPTER IX.

LOCH TRIALAVAL AND THE YOUNG GEESE.

THERE is one point I forgot to touch upon in dissertation on artificial floods, and it is this: that in a downright dry season you cannot do as much as you would like with them. You may assist, but you cannot counteract Nature. In a regular dry season you cannot get up an artificial flood, for the very springs dry, the lochs get low, and, as very little comes into, very little can go out of them. Very great care, then, should be taken to husband every drop of water you can command, and to let it off at the right time—*i.e.*, when the fish are waiting for the water at the mouth of the river to meet the tide, and the wind is in the right "airt." For, with all the water in the world, the fish won't take the river with the wrong wind, whatever that wind may be. Now, as, unfortunately for fishermen in all countries, the latter end of spring and most part of summer are dry, except in large rivers, the water gets low—witness the Wye and the Usk in 1870; and, if dry weather can affect such rivers as these, what must be the effect in the smaller streams? The fishing generally of the western and south-western coasts of Ireland, and those of the north-western coasts of Scotland and the Hebrides, resemble each other much in character, and are equally subject to over-droughts and over-floods,—at one time unfishable torrents, at another masses of stones with a little water. It is to remedy this evil that, if sluices are established, they should be watched with the greatest care as to the proper putting in and taking out; and this is no easy matter, for, if let alone, your true Hebridean, like your true Irishman, smokes his pipe over his peat fire, talks, and relates wondrous tales, but somehow always misses the proper time for attending to his work. Unless you watch him like a rat, your sluices are at sea when they should be snug in a corner out of the rush of the flood, or they are in when some little drop of water should be allowed to dribble out to keep the stones cool. By constant attention, however, we got to know of every available water we could shut up, and contrived little minor floods to get the fish a certain distance up the river Laxay as far as Loch Valtos. I go over this ground too much, perhaps; but my wish is not to delude those who may adopt my plans into the false idea that all is done when a loch is banked up and a sluice put in. No so; you cannot counteract the effects of a decidedly dry season in very, very small rivers. I will add one last word of warning. If you have a good supply of water, never exhaust it, or fancy that, because you have brought the fish into the river, all is done. No such thing. Keep a litle water for them—as much as you can. Poor things! they get thirsty; and bear this in mind, that there is nothing like a little fresh water to make fish lively, which means rising. I have generally found that the fish of the far west of Scotland and Ireland are as fond of refreshment as the natives.

I have already mentioned Loch Trialaval as a great resort of those pests, the gulls; but it also contained other denizens of a much more agreeable nature. The wild geese, who bred in some of the adjoining lochs, Loch Patagore, for instance—though, strange to say, they never did in Trialaval—brought their young there in the early part of the season, for reasons best known to themselves: I suppose to teach them the ways of the world. But, unfortunately, they learnt them too soon after my arrival at

Soval. I had heard and seen a great deal of young geese in my life, but had never shot young wild-goose flappers; and, till then, I had disbelieved in the sport. It requires some arrangement, and lasts about two days, perhaps three. You must here proceed with great caution, for a young wild-goose is not such a fool as he looks, and you must choose the exact time when he can just fly. It is not like flapper shooting, where you have plenty of sedge and cover, and consequently, to a certain extent, the birds lie. It is a species of stalking.

The loch being very large, I generally took two boats, and we proceeded very cautiously to stalk and spy the loch. Having found the geese, we then sent a party or two to secure the fords of the two or three streams that run into the head of Loch Trialaval from other lochs, for which the geese immediately make on getting sight of your boats. Having allowed time for your parties to get round, you get as near as you can without being seen; and manage, if possible, to do as the Prussians did with the French—outflank your enemy and cut him off, or force him towards the fords, when he is headed. If you thus can keep them in the lake, it becomes sometimes a very exciting chase. The old birds stick most manfully to their young, who try to out-swim, and out-flapper, and out-dive you. The old birds don't let their young take to wing, if even they can. They also don't dive much themselves; or, if they do, only for a very short time, and not deep, as they never go far from their charge. Thus they frequently fall a sacrifice to their parental care. Part of the manœuvring is to drive some of the young ones into the small islands that abound on the loch, and then land in them and walk them up; but the real fun is when they take to land somewhere near the fords, and cross the open for another loch. To see a goose flapper along, half-waddling, half-flying, squeaking for his life, is really a very absurd sight. Not so ludicrous, however, as his pursuer, a wild Hebridean, with naked legs and scant clothing, rushing after him with frantic gestures, and yelling out every sort of Gaelic anathema.

I never shall forget an old boatman, poor Callum, and a gaunt, long-legged gillie of mine, pursuing two in this manner, who fairly beat them to a standstill. I never used a dog, except some sensible animal, like Old Tom or Whack, as I think that to do so frightened the birds more than anything. I once got thirty-three in one of these geese battues; but, generally speaking, from fifteen to twenty was the average. It was not destroying for destruction sake, for the birds were capital eating; and what you did not want yourself, were most acceptable to your neighbours. But all things come to an end. My success got wind, and in the spring-time continual searches went on among the natives for the eggs; and at last my friends, taking offence at these inroads, abandoned the country, and my geese battues died a natural death. The natives, and those who should know better, turn the robbery of goose eggs to some account. They set the eggs under domestic geese, and, when hatched, pinion them before they can fly; and if they are fed well, they are excellent food. Also they cross these reclaimed wild birds with the tame goose, and the product succeeds uncommonly well.

So determined were the natives in their egg-stealing propensities, that I was obliged to remove my boats from my favourite Trialaval, for they broke open the boat-house, smashed the padlock of the boat-chain, and although we used to hide our oars, they invariably found them. There is in the Isle of Lewis a species of man called a ground officer, one whose business it is—or is supposed to be—to keep order in his particular district, prevent lawlessness, heather-burning and pulling, egg-stealing, and all petty crimes of the sort I have been describing. Now the ground officer of this district was a respectable farmer and a *soi-disant* particular friend of mine, and I applied to him —with what success may be imagined, when I found out that he himself gave his own shepherds directions to go and smash a new padlock I had put on the boat-chain, and carry my boat and oars off miles away, for the purpose of moving some sheep. There they left it, and it was days before we ever got our boat again. Depend upon it, there are other places besides Galway where the Queen's writ doesn't run. There was also no more determined and successful goose-egg taker than this said ground officer. He reminded me of an old story I heard at Raith in years gone by, of a man driving from Brunt Island to Kirkcaldy, finding the whole road obstructed by quantities of straw, heaps of stones, and all manner of impediments. Among these was a most evil-looking and disreputably-clad man, who abused the traveller horribly for making his way through as best he could. This object accomplished, he turned on his abuser, and assured him that on his arrival at Kirkcaldy he would take care to have him up before the provost. "You maun gang to ——," was the response; "I'm the provost mysal."

On the west side, and about Dalbeg towards Sharbost and Arnhill, there were a good many wild geese, but it was a very difficult matter to get at them, except in very hard, stormy, foggy weather, and I am not certain if the game, even if won, was worth the candle. But exploring Trialaval, which was a very pretty loch, was to me a very great amusement. On some of the islands then there used to be snipes, and I once was in at the death of a hind that we spied and circumvented most artistically. I placed R. M. on the mainland, for which the deer, when moved, was sure to make, and then landed myself on the island and gave the deer my wind, who made for the ambushment, where my friend secured her. The swooping and screaming of the gulls, too, till I destroyed them, was a strange, wild sight to see, and there were always plenty of trout (brown), and in some places sea-trout; occasionally, too, a salmon at the exit of Laxay from the loch. I never went anywhere then without a rod—I should as soon have thought of leaving my flask behind—and I used to bring home a strange medley of things. But times altered much. The geese, as I have said, disappeared; so did the deer, though that was to be accounted for by the foresting of the southern part of the Lews and the northern part of Harris. What deer would stay in the northern part of the island, where they were always disturbed, when they had the South Lewis and North Harris to go to? But why the snipes went I never could account for, except that once I perpetrated an act that must have given offence to the fairies of the place.

I actually gave a party on this Deer Island, as I used to call it, a *déjeuner:* now, it would be termed a garden party. Over the fair waters of my wild Trialaval passed sundry boats, freighted with smiling, handsome faces, determined on pleasure for the day. The old story—"Youth at the prow, and Pleasure at the helm." Not that I was a youth, or had much pleasure left in me; still, I led the way—not in gilded galley, with silken streamers, but in my india-rubber boat, that looked exactly like one of the bottle-nosed whales I have been lately talking about—to my sacred island. We feasted, we made speeches, we gave toasts, we listened to the pipes; all seemed so pleased that even fair hands condescended to raise a cairn to my honour on my island's summit. Unfortunately, we went a step too far—we ventured to rename the island. Alas! my patron fairy took this amiss. Though we all separated enchanted with one another on the evening of that beautiful day, apparently happy and united, soon the scene changed, and strife and discord took the place of peace and harmony. An angry, spiteful fairy can play the mischief if she likes it, and my former friend did this. But what made her drive the snipes away? I never saw one there afterwards. I never had a day's sport on the dear loch again, and there stands the solitary cairn on the lone island. When last I saw it, knowing that I was so soon about to leave my long-cherished home, I felt inclined to pull it down, it seemed such a mockery. "But, no," thought I; "let it stand, a monument of the uncertainty of all human things, and a warning to my successor against indulging in any fond dreams of fixity of tenure. If, however, I ever get a territory again—and I have visions of one in the far north-west of Ireland, where they say there is a river with a lake, with both coble and island upon it—if ever I offend another island fairy by giving another " disjune," as my Lady Margaret

Bellenden calls it, may I be shot at seven times, as I hear the landlord of my supposed territory has been; and, what is more to the purpose, may I never catch another fish, kill another stag, or ride another run with his Grace of Beaufort's hounds.

CHAPTER X.

DICK BURNABY AND GROUSE THE FIRST.

SOON after my removing to Soval, I lost my friend Burnaby. Unfortunately for me, but fortunately for the tax-payers, the survey of the Lews was completed, and he took his departure, to the universal regret of the whole island; for he was one of those who have the singular knack of attaching everybody and everything to them. "Nil tetigit quod non ornavit." The survey is a model of what can be done under adverse circumstances, for surveying and contouring the island of Lews with such a climate is no joke. Looking after his work took him to wild places, and to many of those wild places did I accompany him. Work done, didn't we play and shoot and fish?

We ran entirely in couples. He had a little gig and a small pony, Johnnie, the best piece of horse-flesh I ever knew. He was little over twelve hands high, but, once started, he clattered up and down hill, and never stopped till you reached your destination. Then he was taken out and tethered by the road-side—harness off and locked up in the little gig, for fear of the cows, that invariably eat any stray prize left out—and away we went somewhere. The quantities of fish we used to extract from loch and river, from Gremsta and Blackwater, and other places adjacent, were considerable. I had my own ground. By right of his office of surveyor-general, and by permission, Dick Burnaby roamed anywhere, and I roamed in company with him. F. M. and I then owned half the island, and the rest was unlet, and remained so for a long time, so that Dick and I had a wild world to face; and manfully we faced it. He was a beautiful fisherman, and a very quick shot—very quick, but not steady with the rifle. Seldom was it we came home anything but full-handed. Then he had the merriest, lightest-hearted dog I ever knew, Grouse I., a beautiful black and tan Gordon setter, whom I afterwards bought of him on his leaving the island—a rare dog, whose blood I still have, and prize beyond all other I possess, save old Tom's. Grouse would run behind the trap, with two good otter terriers that never left us; for nothing ever came amiss in our walks. In their company he would chase everything along the road, from a luckless wild Hebridean child to a black-faced sheep, as we all clattered along—Johnnie, Dick, and I, and doggies—in that wild exuberance of spirits which mountain and sea air combined, together with the anticipation of wild sport from an otter to a deer, a snipe to an eagle, a brownie to a salmo, alone can produce.

Arriving at the disembarking point, the terriers came to heel, Grouse resumed his senses, and proceeded to traverse the muir in a style seldom surpassed. Great nose, with sound sense and wonderful powers of finding, he passed nothing. I never could find out whether he was best at snipes, woodcocks, or grouse. He was the only dog I ever saw who laughed when he performed some wonderful circumventing feat. He had a power no other dog of my acquaintance possessed of producing brown owls. This always excited his risible faculties. Once he produced a white one, and then he screamed again, and I thought he would have gone into convulsions. He retrieved everything that was wanted to be retrieved, and cared nothing for a loch in the coldest of days.

Suddenly, perhaps, as we were walking along, one of the terriers would cock one ear, as only a good Scotch hill terrier can (I don't mean a prize Bedlington, or some of the rare specimens of eccentricity exhibited at shows), and look sagaciously at his friend, who would return his observation by dropping one or both of his, already cocked; and then both would start as straight as a crow flies, without a note, for a small loch, distant, perhaps, a mile. In a moment Grouse twigged the game up, and made in a straight line for the said loch, barking for his life in an ecstasy of delight. Away went Dick and I, as fast as we could carry our little bodies (for we were neither of us giants) to the loch too. Arrived there, we found our little friends, each at the mouth of a sort of a small cavern with two exits, one on land and another into the loch, stationary, like two grim little sentinels, and Grouse, half mad, circling round them. As soon as we have got our breath to articulate and strength to enlarge a little the land entrance, with a cheering "have at him;" in goes the land side terrier. A rush and a bustle, and a yelp for the first time are heard, a strange noise, and then, like lightning, the other sentinel at the water mouth is knocked over, and with that extraordinary, springing, demoniac bound he alone can give, a large dog otter plunges into the loch and disappears. Savagely spring Grouse and the

K

terriers after him, and an otter hunt, Hebridean fashion, begins.

Don't be afraid, reader, I am not going to describe an otter hunt; we have no such thing there. I once got two or three foxhounds, and some terriers, but it would not do; the lochs were too many and too large, and the beast always beat us. But if you can get an otter into a small loch, in which you can keep him, with two or three sagacious and real good dogs, you may have some exciting fun in its way; but then it must be very calm, and you must have good eyes.

Our loch was small; Dick took one side, I the other; and at him went our terriers and Grouse, showing, the first excitement over, a sagacity that made up for want of numbers. One of the three always kept the shore, to detect the otter if he banked or tried to quit the loch; the others swam as handy to him as they could. Our office was to watch the otter blowing or venting, and to keep him down by shooting over him whenever he did so; above all, if possible, not to let him leave the loch unknown. Sometimes we lost him altogether for half-an-hour—at one time so long that we thought him gone, when off set the terriers by agreement to his old den, where they recommenced their old game at the find. In went the terrier, out went the otter again with doggie sticking to him. The other settled to as well, and the brave beast dashed into the loch again, with both Skyes fastened to him, soon, however, in his native element, to shake them off. And so the game goes on; but by degrees otter diving even comes to a close. He breathes more frequently, and the dogs get at him now and then; the fights in the shallows are more savage; till at last you see one terrier fastened well between the forelegs, and down go otter, terriers, Grouse, and all, into the loch, and remain so long under that you think they are drowned, till a bubbling commotion is seen, and up surges the half-dead otter, with Grouse and terriers sticking steadily to him, and dragging him on shore, where terriers finish him, and Grouse, as soon as he has got his wind, dances frantically, barking; round a fine old dog otter, twenty-six pounds weight. Oh, blame me not, ye otter heroes of the Wye and the Usk, that in these our parts we so ignominiously slay this game beast! But what can we do? Who would shoot a wild boar that could ride to hog? But, since that grandest of amusements is denied, shooting a charging boar is not to be despised.

T'en souviens tu, mon cher Dick, of these our pastimes in those days of yore, which I believe we both thought the happiest of our lives? The last time we met you were in civilized society; you were quartered on the Curragh of Kildare; your occupation, providing for the defences of that noble camp, erecting sheds for troopers; doing your work well, there as everywhere, and respected by all. But you found something to do there too. I remember we went after some imaginary snipes on the bog of Allen; I don't think there was a fish within miles. But you took to hunting, you dog—and that makes up for a great deal—and you tried Kildare and went well. Do you remember the day you were going so well—a little bit too close, perhaps, for *you* even got jealous—and we took a pull round the crest of the hill so as not to be blown up, when the hounds got hid from our sight for a moment round the hill, and we never saw them again? How savage you were! and I don't wonder, for it is hard to err with the best intentions. Do you remember that day in the park, when we passed so many hours watching that stag near the loch, when the beast would come upon us instead of our going to him, and to get out of sight we had to take the soil and get into the said loch and walk about under its bank—depth varying from the ankle to over the waist—not able to get out for hours or get our shot, and it was not a warm day; and then, when we emerged from our pleasant hiding-place, the animal had moved, and we had to follow him to Larcastal; and at last, after getting a shot and killing your stag, you found him worthless, his horns being rotten? Do you remember this, and then our walk down Benmore afterwards—for Fred had not then made his road up its side—against time to reach our boat before dark, and before the weather came on too bad to cross Loch Seaforth, which it was evidently fast doing, and our passage across without M'Aulay, my gillie being a cur, and yours not much better? However, we got back safe to the Aline diggings. And then do you remember the long, long stalk from Fordmore to close under Diensten bothy, from morn till night, and the crossing that nice long loch, half-swimming, half-wading, with old Finlay M'Lean as our stalker, and lying directly afterwards so comfortably for a couple of hours under that stone, whence we could not move? And at last, getting close up to the stag in the gloaming, and missing him as clean as a riband, you dog, whereat I was wondrous wroth, and swore you should go home to Stornoway that night and get no supper; and even Lochiel blew you up, and said you should be ashamed of yourself, and he would follow your fortunes no more? Do you mind (*Scotticè*) inveigling me one day over to Dalbeg from Callernish, under pretence of woodcock shooting there, ten miles over the muir, getting only one old cock grouse? Then our being confined three days to the house with a Lewis gale, and the nice hailstorms rattling on the skylight windows, and the grand Atlantic tumbling over the cliffs above the house, and our lying down under the spray to watch the breakers. It was a grand sight, was it not? And then the snipes round that quaint little lake inside the sea bay! And at last, when the weather did clear, do you remember the woodcocks round Brahgar Hill, and up the glen and down the haggy flat towards Sebastopol Loch; and then the Carloway glens, and that hillside where you had to cling on by your eyelids to get over the cocks, and how frightfully one always missed them there? And that deceiving Carloway river, with its nice pools, rushing streams, and long, deep, apparently good holding water, in which one never saw or got a fish? Do you remember our snipe-shooting round Stornoway, when we roved where we liked, and nearly bagging two old women close into the huts at the end of the town? And the snipe-shooting at Gress and round Agnish point; and old Alexander, our great pal, who was seldom sober, and never bought and sold when he was, for fear of being taken in? And do you remember the grand entertainment at Stornoway on the occasion of the wedding of one of our friends in the town, when festivities commenced at three in the afternoon with a sumptuous dinner, when everybody made speeches and gave toasts, and swam in Champagne till eight? Then dancing commenced, and continued—with constant *refreshment*, whisky cold and without, or hot and with, or real cold, as the Highlander prefers (that is, pure)—till half-past six in the morning, when you and I, and your dear little wife, turned out of a fine April morning with the sun shining in our faces, not so very much the worse considering; but that under her convoy we reached your habitation, the cottage, in safety. Do you remember all these things now, dear Dick, in your quarters in Halifax? And, as you go in for moose deer and North American salmon, and look after the woodcocks with poor Duke, that I sent you out—

old Grouse the First's grandson—do you ever think of those days and the old trapper that shared them, now a miserable, old worn-out one indeed? Yes, those were happy days, and we were then both merry hearts; we both had cheerful homes, the day's work over, to return to.

> "Two blyther hearts ye ne'er would see,
> The lee-lang night in Christendie."

And there were those who loved to listen to our account of our day's work. And now how changed! Cheerily has gone and goes the world with you, and long may it continue so to do; but you are now a staid patriarch, with pledges to the State for the grave and sober observance of your patriarchal duties, and would not turn out to dine at the governor's in Halifax with Madame, with little Johnnie and his trap, as you used to do at the Castle in Stornoway; while I live almost on recollections of the past—of the light that once brightened my own happy fireside—of the long-loved home, now passed away to others.

CHAPTER XI.

DEAR OLD SHIPPY.

IT was with great regret, as I have already said, that I parted with my friend Burnaby. Independent of the regard I had for him, there was a comfort in having near at hand a countryman on whom one could rely in case of emergency. You may say what you like, but Celt clings to Celt, Saxon to Saxon; and in the far regions of the north-west one likes to be sure of something like fellow-feeling—one wants something like plain, down-right English. Living, as I did at that time, a great deal in the Hebrides, I wanted a companion that understood English ways and habits thoroughly. No doubt, as long as Fred was in the island, and my own immediate neighbour, there was no lack of fellowship; but then, alas! December generally saw him migrate. I don't think I could have stood the island by myself at first without Dick; but when he also went, my heart sank within me; and, but for my bright home, I believe I should have gone too. But Providence was very kind to me.

There still existed another Saxon in the long island—a true one too—with whom I had already smoked the calumet of peace, and with whom before we separated, I entered into the strongest bonds of amity. This individual was the Episcopalian clergyman of Stornoway —whom for short we used, or I used, to call Shippy—and an excellent, good man he was. He was a true specimen of an upright, conscientious being, with good brains, and that rare gift of common sense. By common sense I don't mean worldly sense; but that instinct that sees what is the right thing to do, and never swerves one inch to right or left, to please the "Devil, the Pope, or the Pretender," and thus gains respect, and by respect a following also. His preferment was not very large — one hundred pounds per annum; but then Stornoway was not in those days a very dear place to live in, and its merchants were not "the princes of the earth." The duties of his cure were not onerous, but in their discharge he managed to secure the good opinion of both the Established and the Free Church; and when he left the island to take a small, very small, living in England, he did so to the great regret of all classes. In a pecuniary point of view he did not much better himself by the change; for, while the incomes of both valuable pieces of preferment were equal, the expenses of living in the county to which he moved were trebled. But I advised him strongly to do so, as where he was, with a wife and children, the future was a bad prospect. He took my advice, and that of his other friends, and there he is, "as you was," as the drill-sergeant says, some fourteen years ago, except that he has received some small augmentation of £40 per annum to his means. And yet all agree in sounding his praises as a model parish priest. I visited him the other day on my road north, only to find him the same happy, contented being. Of course his bishop is most anxious to do something for so exemplary a man; but somehow bishops never find the opportunity of doing anything for these plain, hard-working, parish priests. No: tutorise, platformise, inspectorise, and you have a chance. But there are so many good, hard-working men, it would be invidious to select one. It is like the army: the regimental officers get the kicks, the staff the halfpence. Oh, dear! how I wish I was a bishop for only a short time, to give a few good things to such men as good Shippy.

Now, as I said before, Shippy's duties were not of so decidedly overpowering a nature as to prevent my occasionally inveigling him into taking a rod in his hand. Indeed, sometimes I smuggled him out of Stornoway, to come and stay with me, and take a walk over the muir and see my dogs work; and then I wanted to try a gun I had not shot out of some time, and it was taken out by chance, and Shippy came in for a shot. The gulls, too, used to plague his garden, and someone lent him a short, thick single-barrel, that could shoot. But Shippy's passion was fishing, and this I had both the power and the will of gratifying; for, much as I dislike loafers, more do I like seeing a friend enjoy himself by my rivers' side. He was the most extraordinary fisher I ever saw. He did not fish a river—he thrashed it; and there was not much use fishing after him. His lines were cables; his rods something like the good springy twenty feet ash poles we used to jump the fen ditches with in days of yore, when there were fens, and before your improving agriculturists drained them—for which may the unclean beast defile their graves! With these he worked his flies on the water, as much as to say to the fish, "Attention!" and they did attend, and they were astonished at what they saw. For Shippy dressed his own flies; and what flies! I never saw anything like them before, except my own, and they were better; and I did not think it possible I could have an inferior in that art. But Shippy's were even less ephemeral than mine. They were a mixture of caterpillars of various hues, of gigantic size, and rough Welsh buzzes. But Shippy whacked these flies a long way and straight on the water, so that he never missed a fish that rose. His line was never curved—it was always as taut as a hauled-on hawser; and he was a most successful man. I never knew him come home empty-handed, and he used to kill fish when I could not. When he left the island he gave me his flies— if so they could be called—and I killed many, many fish with them, but I never could catch his decided *whack* with them; and no human fly-dresser I ever encountered could put anything together resembling his patterns. He had a peculiarity, too, in fishing. He never could handle a rod without smashing it to atoms; his own poles even could not stand his work. And I used to rig up rods on purpose for him—for I delighted in having him to fish with me—to see if he could break them, which he generally succeeded in doing. But he never came home without plenty of fish; and he was like an otter—he always got the best fish, and seemed always to whack his caterpillars right on the very spot where a taking fish was; for he must have been a taking fish not to have rushed back to sea incontinently on so rough a summons.

Never talk to me about the necessity of fine fishing after Shippy's exploits! I once sent him to the Blackwater with a celebrated fisherman, the surgeon of a war-steamer, stationed for sometime at Stornoway, and a Hampshire man, accustomed to the Test. The sailor boy floated his lines in the air till they, floss-silk fashion, dropped almost imperceptibly on the water. It was a marvel to see, but the product was not equal to the science. Shippy whacked away, and filled his pannier with salmon and sea-trout, and would have filled three that day, I believe; only, of course, he broke his rod, and so badly as to be past mending by the side of the river.

Our friend was not a good shot, much as he enjoyed it; but there was no mistake in his shooting—he missed them clean. There was no feathering, or legging, or following up wounded birds. When he hit them, he did it in earnest—the same whack with which he delivered his flies—and there was no difficulty in finding his bird, or rather what was left of him, which was not much. When he shot a snipe, which did not often happen, the bird vanished into thin air—the long neb alone remaining to tell of what genus it had been. The only thing I ever knew that stood his style of shooting was a wild goose, and even that was not safe to eat after his killing. Occasionally kind friends gave him a chance at a deer; and then was he not in his glory? He drilled such holes through his quarry, that I don't think the Chassepôt could have surpassed his weapon. For all this, Shippy was a charming *camarado*, always cheerful, always full of resource; and I was only too delighted whenever I could get him to accompany me over to the wild west side, to look after all sorts of imaginary things.

Then Shippy had a gig like no other gig I ever saw; a pair of wheels on a very wide axletree, on which was fixed a kind of revolving box, in shape somewhat like the carriages of the roundabouts of immortal memory in the palmy days of Bartholomew Fair. Whether there were any springs I forget now; but, certainly, when in motion, one was not conscious of their existence. The shafts of that vehicle were very wide, and the animal inclosed within them very small, and it consequently rolled in its progress like a trooper-transport in a gale of wind in Table Bay. Dick Burnaby and I were commissioned to horse this wonderful carriage; and, accordingly, we attended the great July fair, then held on the muir side, three miles from Stornoway, on the Callernish road. There we picked out a chestnut pony that would not, it was said, go in harness. This animal, after finding every fault under the sun with every part of its carcass, we, to the farmer's great astonishment, purchased. Dick soon persuaded the chestnut as to the necessity of going in harness, and in due time Shippy was allowed to navigate his own vessel; and I never heard of his coming to any greater grief than pitching a brother, who came up to see him, and was not yet accustomed to its lurches, out on the high road, and splitting his trousers to ribands—he wore them tight and strapped down over his boots. I see him now on the road, near the Creed Gate, as we were going over to the Blackwater to fish; and for the rest of the journey he took a tight clutch of that roundabout. Then the harness of this carriage was not of the highest order; I don't think any of our Lewisian carriages were got up quite in Hyde Park style. But Shippy's harness was really a thing of shreds and patches. The only part about it that could be said to have the slightest substance was the collar; and this having been made for a very large carriage horse, some seventeen hands high, while the chestnut was barely twelve, I often wondered he did not go through it like one of the sylphs through the hoops at old Astley's.

Of course, Shippy, whenever he went on a fishing expedition, as invariably broke his harness as he did his rod. I remember well one night (Saturday), we had been passing the week at wild Dalbeg, and had come across from thence to Diensten bothy, where our respective traps were to meet us to convey us home. Shippy started before me in his, and I was following down the Diensten Hill, in a true Hebridean night, blowing a hurricane, and bucketing hailstones in your face, when through the storm I heard the most frantic exclamations and entreaties not to drive over him, as he could not stir. And there he was safe by the side of the road, with nothing of harness left save the eternal collar and parts of the reins—no vestige of traces. But practice had rendered Shippy very perfect in all mending powers. I fortunately had a dog chain and one or two dog couples, so in less than no time he put himself to rights, and arrived home in safety, though, like Wallenstein's roan that he mounted his cousin on at the battle of Leipsic, "Dog chain and dog couples saw I, never more."

Such was Shippy; and, to me at least, when he took his departure, he left a great blank behind him. We all attended the sale of his effects; and, owing to his popularity, they sold downright well. I remember it opened with some old empty powder canisters, which realised over sixpence a-piece; other things in proportion. The pony fetched twice the price he gave for it; the roundabout three times its value; and the harness—will any one believe it?—realised £2. 10s.

N.B.—It is as well to state that the roundabout was purchased, as well as the harness, by the old farmer I have already written of; who never, as a rule, bought and sold when sober, which was not often. This time he was, and he rued his bargain, for his old pony always took him home on his back safe when he was drunk; but when harnessed, was not accountable for the roundabout's lurches, which very soon nearly demolished his poor old master, and he gave his equipage up.

Thus did the good old Stornowegians show their kind feeling towards the man, and every one tried to possess some relic of one they so truly and justly appreciated. For some time I felt like a fish out of water, my play-fellow gone, and it was not long before I learnt how ill I could do without him. Therefore, should this meet Shippy's eye, let it not ruffle him— as, if I know him, it will not—that I have had my laugh at some of his ways. The object of these reminiscences is to harm or gall none, but to recall happy days engraven on my own recollection, and I flatter myself on that of others; and thus not only cheer up my own decline, but win a smile from those who shared with me those bygone times. The pleasures of memory and imagination being all that are left him, pardon the garrulous old fool if he spins them out to such an extent.

CHAPTER XII.

SETTERS AND WET CRAWLS.

AT last care began to tell, and the grouse increased; and my landlord having kindly raised the roof of my house, I was enabled to take in two guns. By great good fortune I stumbled upon two very nice fellows, soldiers of course—T. D. and W. H. N. by name—who had served and run a good deal in couples together, and delighted in shooting in company. I thus was enabled to gratify my own peculiar fancy, which was dog-breaking—or superintending dog-breaking as I got older, and could not walk up to a pair of young scamperers.

I had taken great pains with my dogs, never breeding from anything but good animals. I had been obliged to give up pointers (save and except keeping up old Tom's blood, of which I always kept a brace), as they would not stand the climate. When I say pointers won't stand rough climate, I must except those that have a foxhound cross in them. They, I think, as far as coat and hardihood go, will stand it as well, or perhaps better, than the well-bred setters of English, Scotch, or Irish blood, whose coats have not the thickness of the ordinary coarse-coated setters. But then I have almost always invariably found the pointer fail in the foot when the ground is wet, as it is in the Lews. The pointer's foot skins and blisters on wet muirs between the toes: but for this, I never should have kept a setter in my life. Indeed, the setters (Gordons) scarcely could stand the constant wet. I never had to do with such a climate for dogs in my life; they were never dry. I never could get them to look as I liked, nor had they ever the condition they should have had. The food was nothing but the eternal oatmeal; flesh was all but impossible to get, and cracklings or greaves are, to my mind, an abomination. There was no bedding but the worst possible description of oat-straw or bad hay. If distemper got among them, good-bye to them; there was scarcely any saving them. Twice or thrice my kennel was so swept, that I almost gave up breeding in despair, when my four best dogs all went in one fell swoop. It was necessary to keep a much larger kennel for my work in the Lews than I ever kept before, as the dogs got prematurely old from the effects of the climate; and, from the impossibility of being properly conditioned, could not do the same work they would have done in other countries. Besides, from the birds being widely scattered, they had to gallop hard, or they were of no use. If a brace did my work for two hours and a half, it was as much as I expected of them; and I generally gave three brace enough every day we shot, which was as often as the weather would let us. I tried every dodge I knew of with my kennels, but I never was satisfied with the appearance of my dogs, though I was more than satisfied with their performance. Though I say it who should not say it, I had a real, good team of dogs, for I never kept a moderate one, or bred from anything but first-rate animals. The real Gordons —I don't mean your show cart-horses, but your thorough-bred racers, compact, sinewy, and bony enough for all working purposes, staunch as steel, docile, and sensible—are a noble breed, and like their old master, well deserve the name of the "gallant Gordons;" and those who have them pure, will rue the day they ever tried to change their real style, and shape, and make. I always took them in hand early, broke them, or saw them broken to hand well myself, and had little trouble with them afterwards with anything but sheep.

Mutton—Highland—they had a decided propensity for, and I don't wonder at it, for a black-faced sheep smeared has an awful scent. A dog runs this scent breast high, when up gets a wild nondescript, whistles like a maniac, makes for the nearest loch, of which in the Lews there are plenty, and into it he plunges like a fool, and then there is grief. I wish the breed was annihilated. Dogs that never notice sheep on the mainland take to them in the Lews. My famous old dog Grouse II., the dog of my heart, I had to part with and send away. One fine morn they brought in fifty-four lambs, which they laid out before the door at Soval, putting their murder to his account. Fortunately, lambs were then not dear, and I left it to the adjudication of three persons what remuneration I should give the people. According to Scotch law, as my poor Grouse had never been known to kill a sheep before, I could not have been compelled to pay anything; but it would not have been either right or politic to have availed myself of this; and, therefore, I had £15 to pay for my favourite's misdemeanours. I have, however, every reason to believe that I was rather done, and my poor dog very much maligned. One of Grouse's judges was the everlasting ground officer, whose two sheep dogs were just about the hour of this massacre out on the *rantan*, as the soldiers say in the district, for sometime. He never said a word about this then, but quietly and secretly destroyed his colleys. This, however, oozed out some time after, but too late to save my pocket, though it did account for the very little uproar the people themselves made at the time. The whole thing, however, did me no harm; my grouse certainly increased, and I never afterwards had a complaint of a dog of mine.

Sheep, then, were the only thing I had to fear, and I never had more than one or two incorrigible instances. One very odd case I must record. The most inveterate sheep-killer I ever had was a very good, staunch dog, very handsome, and a great goer. He had just killed a sheep, for which we had inflicted condign punishment. Shortly after this, the very same day, he went hard at another, and was handsomely running into him, when he turned short and stood like a rock. We went up to him, and killed grouse over him. But there was no keeping him after this, and, to my great sorrow, I sent him to the mainland, where he never showed the slightest propensity for mutton.

Now, never shooting till my two friends went away, which they generally did towards the middle of October, I had ample time to see to the thorough breaking of my dogs, without over-breaking. I was, in short, head keeper. Cameron of Lochiel had long gone, as I foresaw he must, and been replaced by Sandie, who had been a gillie, and accustomed to sheep and sheep-dogs. He had, therefore, like many shepherds, a turn for dog-breaking; and I finished by making him a very good breaker. I had also imported from the mainland (Ross-shire) John Munro, whom I placed at Diensten; I had known him from his childhood; he was a first-rate fisherman, and, having been some time under a good keeper, knew something about dogs, and was not too proud to be taught a little more. He was also a very apt scholar, so that I was tolerably sure of having my dogs well handled. My comrades, too, were good sportsmen, and fond of dogs, and, knowing my hobby, always took care, when I was not out, that order was kept and no liberties taken. To be sure, when they first began, I don't think they were the first shots in the world; had I been a grouse, I should not have minded them much at thirty-five yards; but they mended wonderfully, and one of them, T. D., has since become a very good shot. My two comrades were the two most unexacting creatures that ever existed in the way of slaughter. They were always satisfied with their day's sport, good or bad, and would not even shoot their number if they thought the season would not bear it. The consequence was, our grouse increased; and latterly, when one of the comrades, to my great sorrow, departed, the remaining one and I got on so well together that we eschewed a third, who might have unknown qualities, shot together for the rest of my tenure at Soval, and consequently had very good sport.

It was after the departure of the comrades, however, that my season began. Till the end of October I devoted myself to looking after the few deer that were to be found on my ground, and which, for the first few years I held Soval, did not entirely desert it. There were always a few hinds on the ground that I never molested, and occasionally stags came to visit them, or crossed the ground from the forest to the Monach Hills to the north of Stornoway, where there is very good feeding alongside the burns. It was hard work, for you had long distances to go, and you never liked leaving a stag as long as there was a chance, or daylight to see the sight of your rifle; and some eight or ten miles over the muir in the dark to Diensten bothy was no joke. Fortunately, the ground was soft, so you ran no chance of breaking your legs among the rocks, as you did at Aline, but you might be drowned in a peat hole. Many a tramp had Sandie and I, for he was my stalker, and a right good one he was, for he had been brought up on the ground. I remember once leaving a stag, a good one, that I had wounded, and followed till it was pitch dark, and we found ourselves eleven miles from the bothy. It was as dark as pitch, and how many times we rolled over together—for we walked arm-in-arm—I don't know. At last Sandie said, "Now we must be near the last deep little burn, and we must look out," when "By gorra, you're in it!"—as delightful Lever's car-driver says to Jack Hinton—and into the burn we went, sure enough. Well, we picked ourselves up, and fortunately it was for the last time, as we were near home, which we reached about eleven. We were off before light next morning, for we knew our stag would not go far; and there we found him, not fifty yards from the place we left him, as stiff as a biscuit, and a right good stag he was. We caught one of the wild ponies of the country, tied the stag on him, and sent him home under Sandie's care; and, as John Munro and I were walking home together, what should we come across but two other stags. The demon of mischief came across us; we stalked them, and I killed one, a very old stag, with a bad head. I could have killed the other too,—only he was a small beastie, and I never was a murderer, even with the few chances I got on that uncertain ground,—for, as is often the case, he did not like to leave his friend. He kept waiting for him a little distance off, returning, as they will do, to see why the other did not follow; for the poor beasts often get much attached to one another, and consort kindly together till love and jealousy estrange their hearts, just as they do those of their two-legged foes, and then they forget their old friends and auld lang syne, like human beings.

There is great fun and considerable excitement in that stalking over flat ground. I don't pretend to compare it to hill ground, or to your fine hills and glens and corries of the Park and the south of the Lews, and those grand wild Harris hills; but it has its own peculiar charm. You find a stag on ground as flat as a pancake, wet, soft, and intersected with burns, in a place you would say a rat could not approach unseen. Then you spread yourself out like a frog, and wriggle yourself into some burn, through which you progress—depth varying from the ankle to the hip, sometimes the neck. At times your burn takes a turn almost underground, and you have to swarm over the green moss bank, below which you hear the water gurgling under you; and sometimes squash goes the bank, squelch you go into the burnie on your stomach, and are half smothered with water, moss, and black mud. You must keep your rifle dry, never mind yourself. Then, after some pleasant half-hour's play of this sort, on emerging from your burn, looking and feeling like a wet nigger, you find a step further will put you in sight of the friend you are so anxious about. There is nothing for it but reclining pleasantly on your stomach in a splash of water, supporting your chin on a sedgy tussock. Lie in this pleasant, recumbent position, with a keen north-wester blowing over you in squalls, enlivened ever and anon by those pleasant hailstorms that I'll back the Lews against the world for, that hit so hard about the face and ears and hands—lie this way motionless for from half-an-hour to one or two hours, as the case may be; or, should the weather be warm and pleasant—which at that time of year it is not often—vary the pleasure a little and be midged, having either left your midge-veil at home, or not daring to put it on for fear of being seen; and, if you are not then on the verge of lunacy, you are a very patient, well-enduring man.

But everything has its end, and at last you get up to your stag. Aye, no doubt he is a clean royal—a bonnie beastie—and you put your first ball just over him behind the shoulder, while your second grazes the hair just under it. Then you begin to feel you are cold—very —and utterly wretched. You know your stag will not bring up till Glen Braggar stops him. You fumble for your flask; it is somewhere in the burn probably, where you rolled over when the moss gave way. Sandie doesn't speak, but he looks as if he meant mischief; and you could cry, only you are in too great an inward rage. There is nothing for it but facing for the bothy, eight miles off—a keen north-wester and hailstorms blowing in your lug—which you reach despairing. But grouse soup is a wonderful restorative. After such a day and such misery, you may venture on a glass of stiff toddy (as a rule I never take it but cold and without, Ramsay's best old Islay), and you light your pipe. Then you take courage, and you venture to call Sandie in. After a very strong caulker his heart melts and he begins to think it possible that there is truth in your assertion that your fingers did not feel the trigger, and also just possible the big stag has not left Glen Braggar. Another caulker, and he is to call me very early, and we are to be at the glen's mouth as near daylight as possible.

On such an occasion, off we were in the dark—though, if truth were spoken, my valour was fast oozing out at my finger's ends as I rose, and felt all no how, like a washerwoman's thumb on Wednesday morning. I think I wished there were no such things as stags in the world. But your bath is a wonderful renovator, and collared herring is grand breakfasting. We got off in time, and reached the glen before it had been disturbed by any bipeds. After a long, careful spy, which seemed everlasting and to promise failure, my ear was delighted with a deep guttural, "By Gote, there he is!" And there was our friend, just risen and stretching himself, preparing for his breakfast. If he had only been as tired as I was when I started, and lain still some ten minutes longer, we should have lost him, for he was in a hole where we must have missed him. We were, however, a long time getting at him, as the ground was very difficult, and we had a great round to make. At last, however, we did it. It was a long and an awkward shot; but I felt I was shooting for my life, as Sandie's look was ominous. I thought, if I missed that stag, I might be potted and left in Glen Braggar myself, and it was a relief when the thud greeted my ear, and the poor stag fell like a leaf. I never killed a stag in my life that I did not hate myself as I looked upon him; but Sandie was in ecstasy. Of course there never was such a stag before or since, and they were the best brow antlers he had ever seen; and then what beam! And certain sure he was a forest stag, as he had the short hoof of the hill stag, not the long one of the flat north country.

Then he was closely examined, and it was discovered what a wonder it was he had escaped yesterday, for an inch higher must have killed him, as there was the clean mark of the graze of the second bullet. And there hangs the head in my study; and never more shall I have another wet crawl over that dear old Moreval ground. Indeed, it would be to little purpose now, for the forests of Harris and Kenrisort have such natural attractions for deer, and have so attracted the more northern deer, that latterly it was hardly worth while to go out and look for them, and, though there might be deer on the ground, you seldom found them. It is possible that the new forest the proprietor is making in the neighbourhood of the castle, if it gets well stocked, may again repeople the northern part of the island with deer, as certainly, at one time, they were all over the island, and the Monach Hills, to the north of Stornoway, were then celebrated for the goodness of the stags.

Ah, Sandy, dear, how could you so forget those pleasant days of yore, and turn so on "the old trapper," who never did you aught but a good turn in your life, and made you the man you are now? Remember the advice of the beautiful poet of your own bonnie Scotland:—

> "'Tis good to be merry and wise,
> 'Tis good to be honest and true;
> 'Tis good to be off with the old love,
> Before you are on with the new."

But I forgive you, Sandy, dear—I do, indeed,

from the bottom of my heart—for the sake of the many pleasant wet crawls and the stags we killed and missed together; so take care of the poor Fred's-hoof box I gave you on parting, for the sake of the old horse and his master.

CHAPTER XIII.

A TAME STAG.

WHEN writing about deer and stalking I must mention a curious little circumstance that occurred during my stalking adventures. I was once staying at the Forest of Morsgail with the proprietor, who, on a misty, hill-impossible day, proposed a walk to a neighbouring loch. I was much astonished by the head forester insisting on accompanying us, armed with his rifle, to protect his master against the possible attack of a tame stag, that he said had charged him some time ago, and would have killed him had he not climbed a rock, where the animal could not get at him; and he further declared that, as long as that stag remained in that forest, he never would traverse it unarmed, and that, if again attacked, he would assuredly kill the beast if he could; that he was the terror of the whole country; that no one dared to cross the forest, or go into it, for fear of him. Now this stag was not indigenous, but had been brought, when quite young, from a far-off country, with a view of improving the breed of deer. I had known him well in his youth, and frequently seen him since about the forest lodge, where he sometimes liked to get to the gate before you, and make you believe that he did not intend letting you pass. The under forester, a friend of mine, did not much like him. The stag was also very fond of the milking hours, and used to attend them, particularly in the evenings, much to the dismay of the dairymaids; but, till his attack on the head forester, he had never overtly assaulted any one. Of late he had left the neighbourhood of the lodge, and taken himself off to the forest.

I therefore was much amused by the man's anxiety for his master's safety, and, to tell the truth, thought there was a strong dash of humbug about it. Be this as it may, I stayed some days at the lodge, having capital stalking, and, of course, during that pleasant progress, discussing this wonderful beast with the foresters and gillies.

One day I went to some neighbouring hills to kill a stag or two for a friend of mine, who, not able to come up that season himself, had begged me to get him some good heads, if I could. I met his stalker, a relation of my friend the under forester, whom we will call Norman, and I had with me my own keeper, whom we will call John—no fool about a deer, a first-rate shot with both gun and rifle, and about as pretty a fisherman as ever took rod in hand; it was worth while going all the way to see him fish the saddle cast on that beautiful river the Conon, in Rosshire. The saddle cast on the Conon was a stumpy, short tree, which in floods was half covered with water, and the top of it was shaped like a saddle. To this, in high water, you waded, and getting astride the tree, you commanded a very good cast. This was no easy matter; for if you rose and hooked your fish, you could not kill him from your saddle, but had to descend and wade to shore again. I should like to see any one do it and not lose his fish. John never did. After the usual salutations, we proceeded to work, and had not gone far when we spied two or three hinds and a stag.

"Norman," said I, "we are in sight, for that stag is looking straight and steady down upon us."

"Impossible, sir! he can't; but, at any rate, we can get down to that rock" (distant a few yards), "and there he can't see us."

So behind this rock we rolled ourselves.

"He is moving down this way, master," says John.

"Very civil stag, indeed," said I, and I proceeded to load my rifle.

"You had best be quick about it, sir," says John again, "for he is coming straight down."

"What a very queer, accommodating beast!" I repeated; when, in a deep, tremulous voice, Norman groaned out—

"Ech, Lord! if it isn't the tame stag!"

"Well, what's to be done?" was my question.

"Kill him," says Norman.

"I don't want to kill a tame stag; not so hard up for a shot as that; so take my rifle and kill him yourself."

"I would not lay a hand on him for ony sake," was Norman's reply.

"Then do you shoot him, John."

"I would not like to try, sir; you know you have your own rifle to-day, stocked for yourself, and I can't shoot with it."

Here was a quandary.

"You had best be quick about it, sir," again said John, "for he is coming down sharp, and will be very near us directly."

"For ony sake, don't miss him. Take time, for ony sake, and kill him dead!—the ill-fared beestie!" groaned Norman again.

Now this was not pleasant. I am by no means a sure rifle-shot—on the contrary, a very bad one. The two men evidently thought the stag dangerous, and depended on me for protection. I had no stomach for the affair at all; but I thought it better to be a tailor than a cur. I had not much time for further consideration, for the stag appeared over the brow of the hill under which our rock was, and came right down on us. Thinks I to myself, for I have some Tipperary blood in my veins, if we are in for a scrimmage, it's not lying on my face and stomach I'll be, but standing on my feet. So I stood straight up. On came my friend, facing me, not giving me a chance of his side. I was determined, if he kept this position, not to fire till he was so close that I could shoot him through the neck and break his spine. At about twelve yards, I should say, he stood and turned his head, and eyed one a little askance. This gave me a chance, and I fired; and, though he did not drop dead, he was quite paralyzed, and soon gave up the ghost. Great were the congratulations of my two companions, and great was my relief that no harm was done, though not quite content in my own mind with my exploit.

On my return to the lodge, I was much congratulated on my ridding the country of so dangerous a brute, and for some time St. George and the Dragon was a joke to me. Afterwards, however, came a reaction. Had a real forester been with me, this need not have happened, and a fine tame beast, imported from afar at great trouble and expense, need not have been sacrificed. The poor animal only came down to ogle us, as he used to do the dairymaids, and to satisfy his curiosity. In short, my popularity was as short-lived as Beale's and Potter's, and I became a tailor of the worst unionist-and-picketing description. This did not disturb my equanimity, or give me the jaundice. I have often thought what good men would have done under the circumstances—none of your fanaticos who fancy themselves deerstalkers because they crouch behind their stalker's heels like retrievers, but men like Fred and his henchman Macaulay. I have often asked myself, "Were you a tailor or not, for shooting that tame stag?" "Did he mean charging?" My own opinion is he did not. But, certainly, the glare of his eye was very red and angry; and if either of the men had been hurt, "under my hand," as Mercutio says, I might have been justly blamed.

CHAPTER XIV.

THE WOODCOCK AND HIS WAYS, AND SHOOTING HIM IN THE OPEN.

I HAD other amusements, on the departure of my friends, than those wet crawls after stags, or shooting tame ones. I had to finish off the rest of the ground unshot, and that took me to the end of the season, for I never left any part of the ground unvisited. You must not imagine that I got out every day of my life —far from it. About the first or second week in November arrived the woodcocks. I always left them alone at first, and allowed them to settle; when they did, they generally remained for the season. I don't mean to say that if I came across a woodcock I did not shoot him, but I did not go into their glens to look for them. I do not know anything I ever enjoyed more than that winter shooting in November, December, and January, when the weather would let you shoot. To be sure, the days were short; you could not well see to shoot before nine, and it was a sort of twilight—a very awkward shooting light—by half-past two or three; but then we were borrowers of the night in going to and coming from our shooting. By this time doggies and self were in condition, and the world could not tire us, and I believe we could have marched in the famous Light Division of the Peninsula.

Woodcock shooting on the hills is hard work, and you require to walk a great deal yourself—much harder than grouse shooting. With grouse you can stand still and let your dogs beat for you, walking in the direction you want them to cast for you. But in woodcock shooting you must be a sort of dog yourself, and be always handy to your companions; for a woodcock on a hill-side does not always sit well to a dog, and if he gets up out of range you won't easily get at him again, unless you stalk him, which is very hard—indeed, almost impossible. A woodcock, when he lights (on the hill, I mean), almost invariably runs a little, then gets up and takes a little short flight, though you, perhaps, can't see it, and squats again, ready to be off the moment he sees you after him. The best plan is to let him alone, mark the place, and if you are coming that way two or three hours later, try him again, when you may get at him. All my dogs would point woodcocks, but I don't think I ever had half-a-dozen good woodcock dogs in my life.

It was thorough enjoyment to start of a fine November or December morning (when you got one), with a good brace of dogs as handy as pickpockets, and yourself keener than mustard, never knowing when your dog pointed what might not rise, from a grouse to a white owl. Now we were among the sea-beaten cliffs of Dalbeg, or in the Carloway glens, from both of whose hill-tops your eye ran over the island-dotted Loch Roag, and the great Atlantic seemed breaking at your feet; now wandering in the steep corries of Loch Clay, Loch Vallimus, and Loch Brolum, or round Silver Hill, looking over beautiful Loch Seaforth, on Skye and Harris; or stretching through the far Uig Hills, or climbing the steep rocks under Cleisham in Harris, or dropping down dark Glen Scarladale, with the surrounding black jagged hills round Glen Langan frowning on you, and fair Loch Seaforth smiling a welcome on you again, as you left your rugged hills to nestle in her bosom. Oh, they were glorious times! and it is good, indeed, of Providence to gladden the heart of man with such scenes as the Hebrides afford. I am as keen of sport as any sinner can be; but often have I sat down, forgetting there was such a thing as dog or gun, till a cold nose, thrust into my hand, woke me as from a dream. Yes, I loved that life, and not the least that I never found myself among those scenes without feeling a better and a wiser man. It was then one practically learnt the truth of Shakespeare's sermon, the best and truest in the world, save one. The very dogs seemed to enjoy it, and were better and cannier dogs there than on the dull low flats.

But where am I going to? I was writing about woodcocks, and have wandered away. Woodcock-shooting on the open muir, with good pointers and setters, is very good fun. I know the exquisite delight—the first two or three fences happily got over—of feeling "we are away!" as you settle down to the hounds on your favourite grey, that you know will carry you like a bird. I have felt that indescribable holding of the breath as the salmon turns with your fly, and you feel him, and then hold him in those awful summersaults he throws aloft, slapping his head and tail together; dropping your hand to him in the air, and picking him up as he touches the water, just as a good horseman rides over a fence. I have stalked and slain the noble stag, and felt, as all with hearts must feel, the deep reproach of that mournful eye, and sorrowed as we laid the fallen monarch of the glen in his lonely grave by the cairn's side. But these are the grand inspirations of youth—the beau ideal of the Past. Once I remember dreaming a Peri wafted me to Paradise—a strange one indeed!—an immense grass vale, with light, staken-bound fences, watered by salmon streams innumerable, surrounded by blue hills, on which fed endless royals. Visions avaunt! let us be sublunary and rational.

I have shot grouse on the Moss of Monaltrie, and hunted them in Kerry. I have shot partridges in Norfolk and East Lothian, and looked for them in Tipperary. I remember the fens in England, when "of snipes," as old Camden says, "good Lord, what store!" I have revelled in the bogs of Ireland; I have been nearly smothered in the Brüchen of the Rhine; I have wandered miles in the wild heaths and beautiful copse-woods of Westphalia, and right good sport have had; I have shot a good deal in France, when there was game; I have hunted the wolf, and meanly slain the wild boar with the ball; I have assisted—*proh pudor!*—at that abomination of all sports, a German and an English battue. All these sports have I enjoyed and properly appreciated; but for an old trapper, which I am fast becoming, give me a favourite sport—one requiring a remnant of the fire of youth, tempered with the discretion of age—woodcock-shooting on the open muir.

Deer, bonnie brown bird! I have looked for you in Great Britain, where you were few and far between. I knew you well in Brittany in the days of youth. I have followed you in the heaths and beech and oak coppices of Westphalia. How I have seen you missed in the cock-shooting parties in Ireland, when my fun used to be producing a large bag, from "The Professor" (one of old Tom's ancestors)—retrieving and stealing other people's birds! And O Kerry! O Killarney! the little copses in the mountain glens round the upper lake, down which the birds used to come and go; the black valley, Coomb Dhuv, where I have left bits of my legs; the hollies and furze bushes at the head of it; the glorious Caharnies, the beautiful Long Range, the dark Glena; the lowering Toomies, the grand Torc Mountain, with its fine rocky covert; the peninsula of Mucruss, unrivalled in frost and snow—

"And, oh! if there are cocks in this world to be found,
It is there, it is there!

If only you can get leave to shoot—which, of course you cannot (and very properly), unless known to the proprietors. What happy, cheerful hours have I passed in that beautiful country, and among the hills and glens stretching away down to Carra loch and woods, when it was fine, which it was not often.

Now many, I believe most men, like driving coverts and glens with beaters, and shooting woodcocks *à la battue*—I confess I do not; it is, however, fair to say I would not give a straw for any shooting without my friend, the dog; and therefore I prefer small returns where I can use him, to large where I cannot. But then you must have dogs that not only will point a woodcock when they come on him, but understand where and how to look for him. Having such, I know now no pleasanter sport than to start on a fine morning, towards the middle or latter end of November, when the birds are settled in their haunts (not before, or you will drive them away), accompanied by a brace of trusty tykes, such as old Tom and his little son Jock; your ground looking promising, the distant mountains and rippling sea-lochs giving you something glorious to contemplate when passing over unlikely places, and grateful that God has given you such a beautiful creation to gaze on, and health and strength and mind to enjoy and ponder over its never-ending lessons.

Now one thing you must always study in this sport—the weather about daylight. The woodcock feeds, except when the weather is very bad, at night; and with the twilight, according to the then weather, he takes up his abode for the day. If open, misty, drizzling, he will be found in the most exposed places, squatted flat, like a toad on a rock, or among stones; if downright wet, often under a large stone or bank which keeps the drip from him, which, either in or out of covert, he cordially hates; if cold dry weather and cold wind, he likes the shelter of thick heather and rock; if the whole night has been wet and stormy, there is no knowing where to find him. Bearing this in mind, take to your ground accordingly, and leave the dogs to themselves.

"Come, Mr. Tom, none of your swinging casts after grouse yet, if you please; just try these little hillocks round that swampy ground. Ah! I thought so; and your stern down too." And up gets a woodcock, like an owl as he rises—but don't he, before you know where you are, with a flick of his wing all but put that little hillock between you and him?—but, no; you have got him! and Tom, so pleased, brings and lays at your feet the first cock of the season, the beauty of whose eye is not equalled, or the exquisite pencilling of feather surpassed by any of the winged tribe.

"Mr. Jock, what are you doing there, down in the swamp, wagging your little tail, going slowly, and waiting for me to come up? Oh! yes; the brown bird was feeding there last night." And little Jock proceeds to walk after him, round corners, up through the peat hags, and then looks round at you with such a turn of his eye, as much as to say, "Come along, old fellow; it's all right." From the peat hags on we go into a small run of a rain-track, at the end of which the little dog stiffens himself, with his nose towards a sort of hole in the bank, quite dry, with some sedge-grass like a shed roof over it.

"There's our friend, master," says little Jock, "and I think I can catch him if you like."

"No; give him a chance, my boy;" and whizz goes the woodcock in your face and behind you, and, by all the powers! you don't shoot within a yard of him as he dips through the hags; but, fortunately catching a glimpse of him stealing over the flat, you just touch the tip of his wing with a stray shot, and stop him. Loaded: Jock walks up to him, and ascertaining that he positively is there, rolls himself with great glee on the moss.

A word about old Tom's little son Jock. Alas! both father and son are gone to the place where the good doggies go. Jock was by Tom out of a black-and-tan setter bitch of great speed and nose; but having been let run riot in her youth, she was never properly broken. He was a little black curly-haired dog, with a rat tail, just like a small Irish or Norfolk water-spaniel retriever. He was beautifully shaped, as strong as a little bull, and could go fast and for ever. His nose was wonderful, and he would find more game in a day than any dog I ever owned. But he had a peculiarity—a fault, indeed. When he got on an old cock grouse, he seemed to know what a dodgy, wary old scoundrel he had to deal with, and therefore liked, if possible, to get near and keep his eye upon him. This done, he would stop looking at him all day. In the process, however, he sometimes sprang a bird; though, as he generally found three birds for any other dog's one, he made up for it. But with a woodcock it was different. The moment he got on the haunt of one, he waited till you came to him, and then, with a "Come along, slow coach," on he went, and cunning must the bird have been that walked away from little Jock. This, I suppose, was some of his father's wonderful instinct.

"I should so like to try that loch side with the warm covert to the sun; I am sure there's an old cock grouse or two there," says dear old Tom. "Why, you know I am after woodcocks to-day; but, if you like it, you may; only remember, ten to one, the birds will fall into the loch, and it will be cold work fetching them." "Oh, never mind that; only you kill, I'll get them." On he goes; and "Didn't I tell you?" he says, pointing steadily into some thick heather and stones close by the water edge. Up get two regular old stagers (old cocks that won't pair themselves, nor let the younger birds do so), as we used to call them in Kerry, and, to my great satisfaction, over they go, the two handsome birds, but most mischievous vermin, into the loch — such headers! The gallant old dog brings them out as if it were the 12th of August, Jock chuckling and laughing his little fat sides out at his father shaking the water off, and then, with filial affection, kissing his moist face, waggishly adding, "Cold, ain't it, pa?"

"Come along, Tom; I know you can find plenty of grouse there; but we sha'n't have light for the glens, and I must see what is in them." He turns a rueful look at the loch side, and leaves it with regret. "Now, what are you at, Tom, stopping under the hill-top? I know you have no birds." "Yes, master; but I am sure there are plover over the top, and you know I dare not show over it—they are so wild these fine days." And we top the hill cautiously, and get a chance at a lot of plover, out of which, in that righteous way a blaze into the brown is generally rewarded, we get but two birds; but they look so pretty mixed with the others, and they are so good now they have left the sea.

"Oh! Jock! Jock! why won't you leave those sedges alone? I know there are snipes there, but I don't want them to-day. Well, you do look so anxious and positive, I suppose I must go to you; but I know I can't shoot snipes to-day, and I want to get to the glens." "Do come; try, master;" and so Jock makes me kill two or three snipes to him. Still, on his producing a Jack, which of course is missed, I won't stand it any longer, but walk off with the little black dog.

"Tom, what's that in the sky-line?" "Oh, nothing for us." "Let's see though," and out goes the glass. "A fine golden eagle, and I think we can stalk him." "Well, and what good is he to us if we do get him? He does us very little harm, and, besides, we shall never get to the glens." "Now, dear Tom, do let us try; I never did get an eagle, though you remember that one which went out to sea so hard hit,—the one which kept swooping at you that day you would not keep close enough to me as I told you, and thus lost a good chance." "Well, if you like to try, Jock and I will keep quiet behind." And down we go, and crawl and wriggle ourselves over the difficult ground out of sight, and then go on at a slapping pace till we near our eagle; when, just as we are certain of getting safe within shot, a shepherd and his dog blunder into full sight, and slowly and grandly rises the noble bird out of distance, and, poising and sweeping about for a minute or two, soars aloft and disappears in the clouds. "Hang those shepherds!" says Tom, "they are always in the way. Never mind; come along to the glens."

"Now, then, Tom, you keep one side of the

glen, and Jock the other; I'll keep up the burnside." Scramble, toil, climb up to the head of the burn—not a bird! How can this be? We must try the next glen. I should have remembered the wind has shifted since the dawn, when it was dead on this glen. Of course, no woodcocks. But there's Jock pointing on the plain stone flat on the top of the hill above us. There he goes flicking over, and a miss. There goes another, and clear, too. "You doited old man, couldn't you recollect it was soft, misty rain at daybreak? The glens are no good to-day, and the birds are on the flat tops, and as wild as hawks." On we go up to the stones on the hill-top, and there little Jock makes a sudden turn and looks into a rock. Out comes a woodcock, and he's "round the corner, Sally," before you have a chance, unless you blow him to pieces, a process I singularly dislike. Another point, and a fixed gaze of little Jock's into a snug little dry gravelled parlour under a large slab stone, a regular *cul-de-sac*. "You can't hit them to-day, master; suppose we try and catch him." And between us we produce from under the stone Mr. Brown, whose neck, to save time and trouble, we wring at once. Don't scream out, "You pot-hunter!" Nothing steadies and delights a dog so much as taking up a live bird before him. If you doubt it, try netting and shooting birds to your dog, and see which steadies him most. Well, on we work along the hill-top side among the rocks, scrambling along the grass and short heather; very slippery, loose stones rolling under our feet; holding on every now and then by our eyelids, particularly just as a bird gets up close behind us and whizzes down the hill, your foot slipping on a rolling stone as you turn and pull, your shot going anywhere but into longbill.

"It won't do," says Tom; "the birds are too wideawake here; let us face home, and try the flat the other side of the swamp, where we got the birds this morning; we only tried one side, you know, and that not the best." And, accordingly, thither we resort. The old dog is right, there are some there, and we get seven or eight in no time at all, the two dogs working and moving as if treading on eggs, and never throwing a chance away. Thus we move homewards, killing every old cock grouse we come across (if we can), but sparing the hens; and, what with snipes and plover, the bag, though not miraculously heavy, is very pretty to look at.

I am just smoothing down and looking at the

feathers of that beautiful little bird, the jacksnipe, and Tom and Jock are casting away merrily in the direction of the bothy, looming in the distance, when on the loch, about a mile from it, I see something. "Hist! my doggies." And down go father and son, as much as to say, "What's in the wind now? Haven't you got enough? We are very hungry." "Tom, you remember we got a wild goose there once, and I see something." A little circuit, and I make them out clear—wild geese! "We must wait a little longer, Tommy, till it gets dusk." "Well, I suppose we must; only don't go and shoot into the shadow of the geese, as you did that moonlight evening, instead of into the geese themselves—eh, old fellow?" Cautiously we approach, just as there is shooting light enough left; and, as we look over the bank, up dash the wild geese, and we knock over three—scarcely off the water—with the first barrel, and one in the air with the second. "Not so bad, master," says old Tom, after getting them out; "but do let us go home, for we have had a long day, and done very fairly, considering."

And we reach our bothy in time to get comfortably and leisurely dressed, dawdling over a book or newspaper, for half-past six or seven dinner. Jock and Tom's supper is ready, which (after having their feet well washed in good pot-liquor and salt) they eat in my dressing-room. After dinner we retire to our snuggery. Doggums lay themselves on the rug before the fire, and I don't tell you but that Tom sometimes ensconces himself in an arm-chair, out of which it is impossible to turn him, as he says, "I did as much towards the bag as you, and why shouldn't I be as comfortable?" I enjoy my glass of Ramsay's Islay whisky and water, cold and without, and my pipe. Now and then little Jock makes quaint noises about snipes and woodcocks, and old Tom talks to himself about old cock grouse; and so the evening passes on. I finish the end of a good novel, and about eleven turn in, with fervent gratitude to the Giver of a day of such innocent enjoyment, even though it were the last—and yet with a fond hope of a few more of the same sort; and I dream of killing a mixed bag to old Tom, of everything from a jack-snipe to an elephant, and of suddenly finding a third eye in the back of my head, and consequently killing no end of woodcock in the Carloway glens.

CHAPTER XV.

WOODCOCKS AGAIN.

AT one time in the Lews the woodcock shooting was very good. F. M. on his shootings, and I on mine, followed it up most zealously, and we have often agreed it was some of the best fun we ever had in our lives. There was one particular year when he killed 550 woodcocks at Aline and over the Harris ground adjoining, which was very good, and I killed 350 at Soval. One day he killed thirty-seven, which was the most I ever knew killed any one day. Shortly after I was out on my pet Dalbeg ground, when I think I had the best day's sport I ever had in my life—fifty-seven head of different sorts on a short December day, thirty-one of which were woodcocks. I knew I had killed a good many, but was astonished, while heartily devouring a bit of luncheon, to find I had over twenty considerably, and a famous bit of ground to beat yet. "By Jove! we'll beat Fred," I said. And so I ought to have done, for, with moderate shooting, I ought to have killed over forty woodcocks that day; but, as is always the way with me if anxious about getting stuff, I can't. So, for the rest of the day, down went everything else that got up—grouse, snipe, plover, duck, and teal—but I tailored the woodcocks most awfully, or the bag would have been a thing to talk of. As it was, it was a very pretty one to look at. I remember among the cocks there was a rare specimen of what I never saw before—a pied woodcock, white bars or stripes over the wing, a pied head and breast. It was a very fine bird, and very handsome to look at. All the woodcocks and game were put by in what we thought a safe place, when a cat got in and (will you believe it?) picked out the pied woodcock, and the pied woodcock alone, for her prey. Dire and deep were the blessings that cat received. John Munro, my keeper then, who was a bit of a naturalist, with a pretty notion of stuffing, and had set his heart on adding this bird to his collection, said little; but that cat shortly afterwards disappeared.

Well, those times of the woodcocks were merry times; but things don't last for ever, and, for some reason or other, the cocks became scarcer and scarcer every year for the last five or six years of my tenure of Soval, till they dwindled down to almost nothing, and the game-books told a sad tale. I never could account for it. I never killed them down close, as I seldom shot a woodcock beat more than once. Sometimes I thought my little malignant fairy had done it; but, no, that could not be, for they equally lessened and almost disappeared on F. M.'s ground, too. Now this phenomenon —the disappearance of woodcocks for a time in districts where they have been plentiful—is not peculiar to the Lews. I have known it happen in other places; at Killarney, for instance. I remember four or five—nay, more— consecutive years, when these birds there became so comparatively scarce that they seemed about to desert their favourite haunts. I have thought much on the subject, and don't know what conclusion to come to.

There is, or was, in Argyllshire, a very wise man about cocks—a Campbell, of course—who wrote very well on them and their ways some years ago in the *Field*. I wish he would let us have his ideas on the subject. That they do disappear where they were plentiful is a fact; it is also a fact that they come back again. As for wise saws on the subject, I don't much care for them. One, they take the eggs in Norway and Sweden, where they breed and from whence they come. Gammon and spinach! Woodcocks appear in all parts of Europe, parts of Asia, parts of Africa and America, very nearly about the same time. Given Norway and Sweden as the universal starting-point, does it take them exactly the same time to go from Norway to Norfolk that it does to all other parts of Europe, to Asia, Africa, and America? This can't be, and therefore they must breed in a great many other places where there is no egg trade. Now I have an idea, though I don't know that there is anything in it. We know that at particular stages of the growth of trees and plantations the coverts are particularly frequented by woodcocks. Does this particular growth affect the food of the bird, or the soil that produces the food? But how can this affect a country like the Long Island, where there is no wood, nothing but the bare hill side? True, my good sir, but is it not possible (I know nothing about it) that some temporary alteration may take place in the soil of the hill side which may affect the food produced by that soil, and therefore the last year's experience of his feeding-grounds may have warned Mr. Cock not to go there next year?

All this is, perhaps, mere useless coinage of

the brain. Let us come to something practical, which can be apprehended by all. The woodcock's travelling time ranges, I should say, from the commencement to the end of the autumnal equinox. Now autumn, a most delightful time and climate in other places, cannot be said to be so in the Hebrides, or some parts of Ireland. From the middle of September to the middle of November you are sure of one month, if not more, of the most unpleasant weather the imagination can conceive, and the most opposed to migratory operations. For the last five or six years that particular season has been severe beyond measure, and I attribute the scarcity of these birds to their having been driven clean out of their course by stress of weather. But, from whatever cause their absence has proceeded, it has been a severe loss, though I have no doubt the time will come when they will return, just as they have done in other places. For my part, however, I would rather the grouse had decreased than the woodcocks and the snipes; but then I presume they had not offended the fairy, and three or four successive breeding seasons brought them up wonderfully, till, when I left Soval, the grouse-shooting was really good.

CHAPTER XVI.

LEWS CLIMATE AND MIDGES.

THERE are two points which I must here introduce, without which my account of the Lews would be most imperfect; these are the climate and the midges. To both I have frequently alluded; I must now particularise a little more.

I do not scruple to say that the weather is perfectly intolerable. I have lived many years in Ireland, and of those some seven or eight in Kerry, where it knows how to rain, and where I remember once pretty constant rain every day for six weeks; but the savagery (to coin a word) of the weather in the Lews is not describable. A gentleman from the county of Clare—not the mildest climate in the world—once shot a season with me, and had very good sport, which he enjoyed much. I asked him to come again. "Not for five thousand pounds a year," he replied, "would I encounter this climate again. I am delighted I came, for now

I can go back to my own country with pleasure, since, bad as the climate is, it is Elysium to this." It is a thoroughly provoking climate too; for, as a friend of mine, who was with me for a season or two truly said, "The only dry weather in the year sets in with the fishing, and the wet invariably comes in with the shooting season." The late spring and early summer months are generally so dry that the fish often can't get up till the middle of August for want of water; and, as the grouse are not fit to shoot before the beginning, often not before the middle, of September, when the wet season sets in, the force of my friend's remark will be at once seen. It is not that the weather is rainy only, but there are hurricanes of wind, hailstorms with avalanches of hailstones. No two days are alike. Catch a fine day, it is sure to be a weather-breeder of three days' storm. The rapidity with which the changes come on is really wonderful. I have often been sitting at Aline of a quiet night, when a slight moan and whu-u-ush was heard, and in five minutes it was blowing such a gale of wind over Loch Seaforth that you couldn't hear yourself speak. I have seen the air so thick with rain and squall that you could not tell what the loch was, land or water, except that in some gleam of light you could see the boiling foam of the waves. God help the unfortunate boat upon it then! What the wind can be one has no idea of. I have been blown over on foot more than once, and how one ever got home in the stormy nights from the bothy to Soval, without being blown over—trap, horse, and all—I can't tell. I had frequent occasions to go to Stornoway, and I have walked there in days I would not take my horse and trap out—partly out of charity for my poor old horse Fred, partly out of regard for my own bones. The weather materially interfered not only with the pleasure, but almost with the possibility, of shooting; for you may fish in very bad weather, you may stalk in ditto, and you may hunt, but you can't shoot a wild hill country with dogs in rain and storm.

It is this weather that so thrashes and half-kills your dogs. Supposing the day not to be so bad, the night's and the previous day's rain has swollen the small burns into torrents, let alone the rivers. You may manage yourself to get over the stepping-stones, or you may wade through not much over the knee; the unfortunate dogs have, however, to swim—often carried over by the stream and ducked over head. Now, this is not pleasant for even the working dogs; but the poor dogs who have to be led about in this draggled state till their turn comes, suffer for it, and if the days are cold—which, fortunately, in that country they are not—much more than you do yourself; for you have your warm fire and bed, whereas you cannot get good bedding for your dogs. I used always to let them bask as long as I could by the kitchen fire; but they must go to their kennels at last. In short, I candidly confess that at times the climate beat me, body, soul, and spirit, and I was sore tempted to give it up, and would have done so but for my attachment to the place. Thus, I must say the weather is a sore drawback to the Lews. There is one thing certainly in it—it is wholesome. You are never dry; but the wet don't hurt you, though I have not the least doubt it does all animals except deer, which seem to thrive under it, for the venison of the Long Island is the best I ever tasted, and acknowledged to be so by all acquainted with its merits. Dress warm, for you won't be overpowered with too much heat, and never let anything but wool touch any part of your body; live on game, venison, and salmon; drink no wine, but a little very good beer, and a modicum of good whisky, not too much; smoke in moderation; also dance a reel whenever that prince of pipes, the proprietor's piper, is handy; fear God and honour the Queen—and you'll do well, even with the atrocious elements of the Lews.

Ladies and gentlemen, do you know what midges are? If you don't, pray go to the Lews. I do not say they are merely an annoyance, for they are a drawback to enjoyment there, and their presence amounts to such a nuisance that of themselves alone they ought to necessitate a reduction of 100 per cent. on rent. They interfere with every occupation in life. Fishing, you must either be stifled with a midge-veil or smoke yourself sick to keep them off. When you sit down to luncheon, that most enjoyable of hours in either fishing or shooting, they are all but maddening. I have lately described what they can be when stalking, and even on the highest hills they will pursue you, and if they catch you there I think they are worse than anywhere. In short, they are maddening even to the natives, and I have often been fairly driven home by them. Then there are a few of those delicious days that sometimes come even in the Lews, when the *dolce far niente* is the only enjoyment to be had. You saunter out to wander by the river side, or sit down to watch the sea loch softly rippling to your feet, delighted to have such a scene to ponder on. Not a bit of it. The tempter of all has even there his infernal machinations at work, and from the bottomless pit sends forth his demons in the shape of myriads of midges, to scare all good thoughts away and drive you frantic. Or you stroll out on a fine evening with your lady-love, to show her some of the beautiful points of view, or your pet casts in the stream, and you watch for the expression of those speaking eyes. Don't you wish you may catch it?

You have been obliged to wrap her well up in a midge-veil, or the said eyes will be closed in the morning—bunged up, as we used to say at school—with midge-bites; and a blackamoor's lips are a joke to what that sweet little mouth would become. A muggy, calm, hazy, drizzly day arrives, unfit for any outdoor amusement; you settle yourself down in your bothy to improve your mind or write your memoirs. Vain effort! The windows have been opened to let in the air, and the midges have taken advantage and come in too. Your den swarms with them, and your only chance is to light a peat fire outside the windows, perhaps on the floor too, and fill the house with peat smoke, or be midged. Pleasant alternative! For the after-reek of peat smoke is not nice, and that same being midged is no joke with some people. I have known individuals so punished that it has brought on fever and erysipelas. I don't care for the insects as much as most people, but once I had erysipelas from midging, and was laid up for some time, and at another time a downright bad leg, which bothered me for weeks; and I do not hesitate to repeat that in the Lews they amount to a positive plague. The best preventive is either a midge veil or smearing your face and wrists well with stag's grease, not the pleasantest thing in the world. Oil of thyme is nicer, and will sometimes do, but you must keep repeating it. After midging, I found the only soothing process was to bury your face in as hot water as you could bear.

CHAPTER XVII.

STORNOWAY.

AFTER all I have said of the Lews I must not forget its capital, Stornoway the magnificent, the London of the Hebrides; the city of merchants, the grand emporium in those northern climes of cod and ling, herrings and haddock. It beats the world, and Dublin Bay to boot, for the haddies, and everything for the herrings except Yarmouth and the Dutch coast. How cheery and pleasant it looks of a bright morning, with its white houses in a sort of amphitheatre round the bay, and up the rising ground above, flashing in the sun as you sail in; the castle standing well to the left, a good feature in the landscape, till they spoilt it by tacking on a wretched conservatory, Crystal Palace fashion, to it. Who the mischief ever saw a conservatory hanging on to a baronial castle, like a Chinese pagoda?

When first I knew this great capital it was a

nasty place, redolent of anything but the sweets of Araby, badly lighted, wretchedly paved and roaded, with such mud and such holes! But now it is very much improved. There is a nice pavement in many of the chief streets. It is lighted to a certain extent with gas. It is made now a Scotch burgh, and there is, I think, a corporation. The inhabitants and the proprietor fell out about the foreshores and the quays. Who was right or who was wrong I never could make out, but they settled it, I presume, to their mutual satisfaction; and the town certainly progresses, and is assuming every year a neater and cleaner appearance. I believe the inhabitants are very much indebted to that very excellent and systematically improving lady, Mrs. Percival, who is there, as she ever has been wherever her lot has been cast, as active as she is judicious and benevolent in all she does. There is a Freemasons' Hall, a good room, in which many is the reel I have seen danced, and awful the quantity of toddy imbibed. Underneath the said hall is, or was, a billiard-table, at which the Stornowegians played their matches. So curious a specimen of what a table can be I never saw. It was not large; for, had it been, no human arm, with the strongest cue, could ever have pocketed a ball. Even as it was, but for a certain natural attraction in the pockets, large as they were, taking up a considerable portion of this table, this feat never could have been performed. The surface was not slate, but a sort of wooden ridge and furrow, with deep holes, covered over with very rough baize. The balls were very large, corresponding to the pockets. The only plan of making a hazard was to hit your ball very hard into one of these holes, out of which, if it had force and way enough, it made a sort of ricochet, and hopped over in the line of a pocket, which, if it only landed near enough, was sure to engulph it; for never had even Scylla and Charybdis such powers of suction as these pockets. It was rather a service of danger looking on at one of these matches; for the room not being very much larger than the table, if one of these cannon-balls in its bound cleared the pocket, and took you in the pit of the stomach, which it sometimes did, it would have knocked you over, but for the wall, that brought you up standing. Dick Burnaby was a tremendous hand at this table, and, had the play been high, he might have ruined Stornoway; for he was a good player anywhere, but at this table invincible. Fortunately, "the tables" were the highest stake ever thought of, and I don't think Dick's play ever cost him much.

There was in Stornoway a very excellent school, both for boys and girls; and I was really astonished, though having some experience in good schools, at the manner in which the children of both sexes acquitted themselves. The needlework of this school exceeded everything I ever saw, except the famous school of Clonakilty, I think, in the county Cork. For this school I believe the town to be indebted to Lady Matheson. There was also a corps of volunteer artillerymen. They said the practice was good, but I never attended. Unfortunately the privates were armed with very good carbines, with which, if they did not shoot deer themselves, they lent them to their friends in the country to do so. My watcher took a native with one of these weapons, which was traced to a corporal, I think, of the corps, a most respectable man, of course. With true Hebridean, perhaps usual, justice, they punished the poor set-on devil, and let off the real Simon Pure, because of his being highly connected; instead for that very reason punishing him the more severely; as an Irish judge hung a gentleman, precisely because the grand jury recommended him to mercy on the score that as such he ought not to suffer. They look well under arms; and may it be long before their prowess is tested.

There is one custom in Stornoway that I must allude to. Whenever any one has lived some time there and is about to leave it, be he a native or a foreigner, if he is popular, he is invited to a farewell festival, not a dinner with speeches, &c., but a festival, and so lugubrious a one I never witnessed. A funeral is far livelier, particularly if it be given in the Freemasons' Hall, as it frequently is. The inviters are all seated on the benches round reaching up towards the roof. In the centre, or rather before the benches, sits the invited by himself in a high-backed chair, like a culprit. Nobody says a word—nobody laughs—every one looks as solemn and glum as at a Quaker's meeting till they go mad. In solemn silence do the entertainers imbibe their grog. At last on a signal given or word spoken, the Benchers arise, and in a tone more awfully solemn, and more peculiarly grating even than the old intonation of a psalm, without organ or key-pipe, they drawl out "Auld Lang Syne," till one almost goes melancholy mad. I know I nearly did—more particularly when I remembered how in days of yore, at Cambridge, we used to give it out from Barnes's Rooms, in the Old Trinity Tower, myself sometimes leading the voices, till one night we roused old Bishop Watson, the then Master of Trinity, from his slumbers, and he sent the porter to bid us dismiss our company and depart in peace.

Pardon me, my dear reader, but you know my desperate, digressive spirit: I must bring in here a little story of that memorable evening. My dear old friend—the best, the pleasantest, and the cleverest man of the day, the soundest lawyer in England,—was among the party. He demurred to the porter's summons, and sent, through him, his compliments to the Bishop, to say he protested against this interference with the liberty of the subject. The porter returns with an order to the recusant to attend the Bishop personally and immediately. E. goes and appears before his lordship. Interrogated as to the reason of this extraordinary uproar at such an undue season of the night,

"No uproar at all, my lord," retorts E., "only a few lovers of liberty assembled together, and we have been singing 'Scots wha ha'e wi Wallace bled.'"

The Bishop, who was a scholar and a wag—
"Then, Mr. ——, as you are so very fond of

liberty, please to translate Æschines' oration on the Crown."

This my poor friend did so beautifully, that the Bishop, whenever he saw him, always inquired when the friends of liberty met again, that he might have the pleasure of reading his translation of Demosthenes on the same subject.

After this story, can any one wonder at my sensations at hearing that fine old song so murdered? and one felt inclined to roar out, "Hold hard, for anybody's sake, and let me teach you how to sing!" But you can't disturb a Scotchman's gravity. It ain't in him to be cheery; and, barring Burns, I don't think Scotland ever produced but three real cheery coves—Willie that "brewed the peck o' maut," and Rob and Allan that "came to pree." As it is, Heaven defend me from ever again assisting at a Stornoway soirée.

To be sure, there were blither entertainments in that celebrated capital. When the castle was lighted up, the rooms and corridors, and staircases decked out—above all, that beautiful ball- and music-room thrown open, which used to remind me so of Almack's in its palmy days when I was a boy, and the Redouten-Saal at Vienna—it was a pretty sight to see. Well did the hostess, the Queen of the Isle, do the honours of her ball. All Stornoway was there, dancing with that grim determination Scotchmen alone can put on such festive occasions. And how they do dance! In that very extraordinary, and when well done, beautiful dance, a Scotch reel—the dexterity and neatness with which the evolutions and steps are performed, has oftentimes perfectly astonished me; as close-packed almost as herrings in a tub, they never jostle one another, or get into any mess. I have seen more confusion, more sprawling about, in a London ball-room—aye, and less manners too—than in many a Scotch dance in a barn. And not only in their own national dance is it that they so excel; but see them dance a French *contredanse*, waltz, galop, or polka, and there is none of that rough horseplay work you so often see in England.

What is it in the Highlander that makes him generally so well-bred and civil-mannered a gentleman? It must be the remains of the clan education; for though, from the complete revolution of property that has been progressing for years, and still, alas! progresses, clanship is gone, or fast going—yet still a M'Kenzie claims kindred with high Kintail, and must not disgrace his name. Supposing you lived near to a small provincial town in England or

Ireland, and invited all the respectability of the town—the doctors, the lawyers, the hotel-keepers, and the exciseman, together with the chief of the respectable shopkeepers—to a ball, and gave them before supper plenty of the refreshments I have elsewhere spoken of, an excellent supper, plenty of champagne, and all sorts of liquor—I rather think after supper the dancing would be uproarious, and many of the company decidedly the worse for drink. Indeed I have seen very fine balls of this description in fine English provincial towns, where some of the company had to be ejected; but I never saw anything disagreeable occur at any of these Stornoway balls. Though they liquored handsomely, they carried it like gentlemen, and only danced the harder and the better. It is this quality that enables the Highlander, wherever he is, and whatever his success in life, to rise to it. There is a quiet sort of dignity about him that always sets him at his ease. He may be pompous—he may swell about in his tartan hose and philabeg, as if the room was not large enough for him; but he is never vulgar. "Il ne vous agace pas les nerfs," like your genuine English snob; or the clipping-the-King's-English Hibernian. The Stornowegian ladies are exceedingly well-mannered, gentle creatures; but then Scotchwomen, as a rule, are nice, and they really do love dancing for dancing sake; and you used to see their eyes glisten again as Thomas McKay, Sir M.'s piper, blew up the pipes for the Reel of Tulloch. I believe he would have warmed up even the givers of the farewell soirée I lately spoke of with that reel.

A word about this said piper, for he is worthy of it, and was a great ally of mine. He was a slim, handsome fellow, as many—perhaps most—pipers are. He had one of the best figures I ever saw, with a quick, ready, glancing eye, that could take any humour it pleased; I never saw a more naturally graceful creature. He was a universal favourite: as for the women, I never saw one, young or old, that did not turn to have a look at him as he passed, and the more they looked at him the more they liked him. There is some old song ringing in my ear that I have heard sung somewhere—

> "Oh wasna he a Roguie, a Roguie, a Roguie,
> The piper frae Dundee."

Now, don't mistake, or fancy that "roguie" means a rogue—"roguie" means a good, dear, insinuating, pleasant, light-hearted, devil-may-care kind of boy—something like Juan before the women spoilt him, and he became too bad. But then my piper had more good qualifications than his pipes and his good looks: he was a Jack-of-all-trades, and I believe there was nothing he could not do. Of his fishing powers I have already slightly alluded to. He was a surprising fisherman. To look at his ordinary cast before you, you thought he was sniggling or dibbling a fly at a chub; but he always twitched it up so that it was as straight as a poplar, and woe betide the fish that rose at it. Watch him when he was fishing and no one looking on, and he would send his fly as far as any one I ever saw—barring only, as I always say, old Daice. He was by way of looking after the Gremsta, having his domicile close to it, when the family were away and he was not piping at the castle—and he had permission occasionally to kill a fish for his table. This permission, it is believed, he used very much as the Clerk of Copmanhurst used his to kill an occasional buck in merry Sherwood. As you went up the river, or to the best casts on the different lochs, you would often descry a light, tall, airy figure, with something uncommonly like a fishing-rod in his hand, flitting away from your pet cast. He had the two best otter terriers in the island, and a handy little gun; and certainly the Gremsta was not burthened with many of the said amphibia. Men did say (but that might be calumny) that he was a first-rate stalker, and the head of the Gremsta lochs was not very far from Kenraisort Forest, and Fordmore was a great place for deer; and as it was his duty to be often at said Fordmore, to guard that fine salmon-cast and pass for deer, it was of course his further duty to look after said deer; and if he occasionally looked after one for himself, where was the harm? As if one would not have done so for oneself. I should, for a certainty.

There was one great qualification, too, that this piper had. He was a wonderful cook; and, as he was generally selected as the servant to accompany the gentlemen who went stalking to Kenraisort when there was only a bothy there, and before Morsgail was built, his fame as an artist was widely spread. He concocted the most delicious stews. I could not conceive how or where he learnt his art, but at last discovered his plan. He stewed or heated up the contents of one of Hogarth's, or some one else's, tins of preserved meat, in Harvey's sauce. He boiled potatoes wonderfully. He scored and toasted sea-trout to perfection, basting them the while with butter, and peppering and salting them well; and he did venison steaks (the only way to eat red deer venison) to perfection. You may judge he was a keen sportsman, and somehow we cottoned; but he had the queerest, though not the pleasantest, way of expressing his approval of any of your proceedings I ever rememember. I had been sent to Kenraisort to kill a stag, and the weather, as is not unfrequent in the Lews, had been of that atrocious character that shin-burning—while reading and re-reading the two or three books one had—was the only order of the days one had to pass inside that bothy. Besides, the wind was foul: the Harris lochs, Washermit, Scoorst, and Uhlevat, were over their banks, and not fishable. Three days of this pleasant weather had passed over, when, on the fourth morning, which seemed worse even than the three preceding, Angus McLean, the Kenraisort stalker, came to say the wind was changed, and that we must try for the stag, as he was wanted at the castle. I obeyed orders, rather against the grain, only I had not pluck enough to say nay. We sallied forth on one of the worst Lewisian mornings, which is saying a great deal, of my experience. Blinding hailstorms; squalls that you had to hold on not to be blown over—and Heaven knows where, for we were on the high ridge of the point over Loch Langavat. During the occasional gleams of light that break out by fits and starts in those bad days, and were signs of their not improving, we got sight of a stag lying on a ledge of rock, sheltered by another by his side, with his head stretched out, and thus lying snug. Stir we could not, and were obliged at once to take to the lying-on-your-face-and-stomach position, which was remarkably pleasant where we were. We lay there more than an hour, and I am glad now we did, for I learnt what squalls could be. I thought Loch Langavat would empty itself bodily over the top of Rohneval Hill. Had I not seen what I did see, I could never have believed it. At the expiration of an hour, or more, I rebelled, and swore to Angus that lie there any longer I would not, but must try a shot. He consented to my wriggling myself a little further, which I did, and got a very little more above my friend. The case seemed hopeless. I had nothing to shoot at, with any hope of success, but the backbone towards the shoulders; but I felt that human nature could not hold on much more, and that I should shortly be blown over into Loch Langavat, or what remained of it, and thence over Rohneval. I was utterly reckless, so I took a short aim, for the blinding drift was too much for a long one, and pulled. To my great astonishment, as well as that of Angus, off his ledge rolled my friend, as dead as a herring. He was a very good stag, an old one, with the quaintest head I ever shot—one very thick, long horn, another short, stumpy, but very thick one. The gralloch, as you may imagine, did not occupy a very long time, and we ran home as fast as we could. We had not been more than two hours away. The piper greeted me on my return with kind condolences on the weather and on my endurances, and proposed the hottest of toddies at once, for which he, with great forethought, had the kettle already boiling; and he went on discoursing on the uselessness of disturbing ground such a day. "But I've got him, piper." He started and stared, as I once saw him do on the only occasion I ever knew him lose a salmon, and turned round to Angus for confirmation of my assertion. On Angus nodding assent, he said nothing, but at once gave me a lounder between the shoulders that I believe at the time restored the proper circulation of my blood, and sent it from the head to the extremities, but which I shall not easily forget. I once experienced another. After Christmas festivities at the Castle, I had to start early one morning by the steamer for England, and Thomas, who had been my attendant, saw me and my traps on board. Whether the tip exceeded, or did not come up to, his expectation, or whether he had had an unusually strong *morning*, I don't know; but he gave me a second parting lounder, and, though I know not what sea-sickness is, I was qualmish the whole passage.

One more trait, and I have done with this king of pipers. I arrived late one Saturday evening at the Castle, after fishing in the Rock pool at Laxay, and had round my bonnet a very good casting line, with a rough red Welsh buzzy fly—a capital one for fish late on in the season, particularly for the last arrival of fish fresh from the sea, with sea-hue on them, fair in colour, but just ready for spawning. (N.B. I always returned them to the river when I caught them.) The fly was also very good for the large red fish who came up early, but who never spawn, or never meant spawning, this year. They seldom rose, but, when they did, fought like demons, and, when killed, made capital kippers. Of course piper was in attendance, and I told him of my success, for I had had very good sport. There was no time for talking much, as I had barely time to dress for dinner. I had taken my cast of flies off my bonnet, and, as I thought, hung them on the looking-glass; but a pleasant party and other avocations made me forget all about it; and I went away early Monday morning with my bonnet, but not my flies. I missed the cast much, but forgot them again till my next visit to the Castle, when my piper asked me if I had not lost a cast of flies; on which, on my replying in the affirmative, he produced the missing one. I shall never forget his demure face, for the fishing season was now over, and the piper could dress a fly. Of course I gave him two or three good flies in return for my buzz, for it was the best I had; all I said was, "Keep it to yourself." "May be, I won't," was the reply; and I never saw any one else with the buzz.

There is one very busy time of the year in Stornoway, and that is during the herring season, commencing generally early in May, and continuing through that month and through June; sometimes through part of July. At that particular season herring-boats rendezvous at Stornoway from all quarters; and it is a very pretty sight to watch of a fine May or June evening the herring-boat fleet go out for their fishing. They return in the morning, of course, with varied success. The fishing boats come from all quarters—from France and the Baltic even. Of course the majority are English and Scotch. A great many live in these boats; many also for the time lodge in the town, where they are taken in and done for.

There is one very singular class of persons attached to the fishing boats, and that is the fish cleaners, or rather gutters. They are mostly females. They do not live on board the boats, though some are attached to them; they never go out fishing with them. The fleet generally returns in the morning after fishing all night, and then begins the cleaners' work. There are along the different quays which are attached to the different houses of some of the chief fish merchants, temporary sheds established, and in these the fish-curing commences, and very expeditiously is it carried on. Herring gutting is no clean, pleasant, or savoury occupation; but it is very expeditious. With bare arms, feet, and legs, and not the greatest quantity of coarse clothing, these ladies set to work, and the expedition with which they prepare a herring for salting would rather astonish the most expert of London oyster openers when there were oysters to open. Their work got through, they breakfast or dine, and then commence the most elaborate toilet. Among them you will often remark exceedingly handsome women, of that dark, Spanish type that you sometimes see in the Highlands and the western parts of Ireland, only I never could make out why. When dressed up in their garments of many colours, rich and gaudy, as they lounge listlessly about the town, they form a strange contrast with the rest of the population. They seem, like Portobello and Musselburg fishwomen, a race of themselves. They often have that dark, flashing, glistering eye that speaks what they might be if offended; and as they say they never leave their knives behind them, on giving the slightest offence, you might in a twinkling find yourself made a herring of. But I never saw or heard of anything among them but the most orderly and respectable behaviour.

There is one particular attending this herring season by no means pleasant. The refuse of the fish remains about the quays, sheds, and curing-houses, and is carted away as manure, and very excellent it is for the fields in the neighbourhood of Stornoway; but the odours of that great capital are not, or were not, improved by the process; and for preference I should not go to town for the season, were I a Lewisian, at that particular time of the year.

The herring season was the stirring season of Stornoway, which at other times was not exceedingly animating. I had many friends there, who were always most kind and hospitable, too much almost for one unaccustomed to their mode of life. Stornoway is not given to early rising, and when I come to describe life there, this will be accounted for.

Whatever Scotch breakfasts are in the Lowlands and in the grand Highland counties, certainly in the far north I can't say much for them. To make a good breakfast you must have good provisions; and in Stornoway, unless imported, they are not first-rate. And whatever people may say, salt-fish, and ling, and cod, and Scotch ham and eggs, are not exactly appetisant; and so I presume the Hebridean thinks, for he is never in a hurry for his breakfast. Wise man! he knows what it is going to be. Therefore you seldom see it before ten, and then, in order to prepare for it, you are, before setting down, invited to some bitters—*i. e.*, a stiff glass of whisky with something in it, bitter and detestable enough to set your teeth on edge, and which does so astonish your poor little stomach that nothing it can possibly partake of for the rest of the day can do so again. Having got through the meal as best you can, towards eleven, or perhaps earlier, you proceed to make your calls of either kindness, pleasure, or what not. Wherever you go, and particularly among your friends, you are asked to take some refreshment. Now, refreshment means one (at laste, your honour) glass of whisky, neat if you like, or with as little water as you like. To refuse would be a deadly affront, never to be forgiven. Now, supposing your acquaintance to be large—mine was (for Soval being on the highroad to Harris, I might as well have taken out a license, and put up my arms on a sign-board, for every one going the road rested himself there)—you took in a good deal of refreshment between twelve and four or five o'clock, when dinner took place, to which you sat down with a sort of whisky appetite—that is to say, none at all. You got breathing time during dinner; for the true Highlander, like the English labourer, eats his dinner first and drinks his liquor afterwards. After dinner two tumblers of toddy are the general allowance. But the tumblers are large, and therefore two glasses of whisky are required in order that the *miller should not be drowned;* and, as a new fashion has been introduced—

that rum improves the taste of the toddy—round goes the rum-bottle. Mind, you don't diminish the whisky, but you add a glass of rum. This makes a decidedly strong caulker, of which two are enough under ordinary circumstances. About seven or so, you go up-stairs to tea, and rest on your oars a little till about eight. Then one or two people drop in, and, of course, one refreshment takes place, shortly after which you sit down to long running whist, and Lord! how well these Stornowegians play! They never forget a card, or make a mistake; fortunately they play low, or you would be ruined. Not that you might not play with them in the dark for guinea points and a pony on the rubber; but they play so infinitely better than ordinary mortals, after such a day's refreshment as I have been describing, can possibly do, that the side must lose where one of the partners is a southerner, not accustomed to it. During the rubber one or two, or more, refreshments at least take place. About ten comes in some sort of supper—I don't mean a good devil or a broil, but a something to eat; and afterwards follows unlimited toddy till you retire for the night, with such very confused notions that unless you are a Stornowegian, or well broken into the ways of the place, you would, as quoth the Baron of Bradwardine, be decidedly pronounced "tametsi ebrius." Now, this sort of life is all very well for once in a way, but for a continuance would give any one but a Lewisian delirium tremens. So it will be imagined I eschewed Stornoway, except on occasions when I could not help myself.

CHAPTER XVIII.

SUPERSTITIONS.

BUT after the different things I have said of the Lews, some account ought to be given of the quaint superstitions and stories of that country. I am not going to touch upon any part of that field of second-sight and Highland seers so ably described by many other writers; but suffer me to tell two or three stories, or rather meander away upon different stories and incidents that came under my own immediate knowledge.

Now, I don't pretend to be a hero in the dark; I had rather walk by day than night any time, and I don't think it at all pleasant being by oneself in a lone corner of a house or muir —above all things, on a good high road in the neighbourhood of a large town, manufacturing or otherwise, between twelve and two in the morning—say from the "Peacock" at Islington to the Edgware Road; or from the Regent's Park country to the top of Portland Place. But still, if the thing is to be done, it must be done. I have never exactly made up my mind about ghosts, but I don't see why they should be an impossibility; and I don't believe, if the truth were really spoken, that any one quite alone hearing a strange noise at night, or seeing a queer sight on the road, that he don't feel his heart beat, and would not sooner have a comrade with him. I don't think that he is quite as cool as he would be in the broad daylight; and absolute coolness and indifference are the criterion of courage according to the old French soldier's view. In the Moscow campaign, when France had soldiers, two of the Old Guard had a bet on which was the coolest under fire. They decided the wager the next day—I think, if my memory serves me right, at Borodino, where the fire was heavy enough to please any epicure. "Tiens, tu as perdu, mon camarade! Regarde—il déboutonne l'habit." Latour Maubourg had unbuttoned the top button of his coat. His comrade demurred to this, and the decision was referred to a committee of old soldiers, who decided that he had lost. Latour Maubourg evidently felt hot, and Poniatowski did not. Nobody, they say, is a hero to his valet-de-chambre, much less to himself. What is the use of it? No one is a bit the wiser.

"Why should I bribe myself?"—as said a celebrated English Prime Minister to a friend who asked him why, at least, he did not give himself the Garter.

Therefore the result of my lucubrations is, that being conscious of being no hero in the dark myself, I have a fellow-feeling for those who dislike it too. But, then, there is a limit to all things, and I don't think that generally ghosts walk till past ten at any rate; so you surely need not mind them, however much you may other bipeds, who are more dangerous in the early than in the late hours. But, then, if you fear the swell-mob in the early, and the ghosts in the dark hours of the night, you won't have a cheery time of it anywhere, particularly in the Lews, when your dusk certainly begins about four in the afternoon, and it is not light at eight in the morning. Now, I have met with a good deal of fear of the fairies in the far west of Ireland, and consequently imbibed a great respect for their reign; for the Irish fairies, like some other inhabitants of the land they are said to frequent, are mighty pugnacious, and often administer a hearty drubbing to those who interfere or go out to dance with them by the light of the moon—at least, so I have been credibly informed by the fairy dreaders; for I never met a fairy myself, by day or by night, though I lived a long time in their peculiar land—Kerry.

But for true night-fear commend me to the Lews. Very few, indeed, ever ventured on night-travelling, and that only in troops. I had a very excellent workman in my employ almost all the time I was at Soval. He cut my peats, did all my farmwork, which consisted chiefly in keeping up a turf fence round a field that produced nothing but a small crop of rushes, though it had been drained in every possible manner. This turf fence was always cracking and crumbling back into the field in the dry weather, and tumbling down into the ditch and the road or the loch in the wet weather. On the whole, I never knew what good the field did any one but poor Callum, to whom it afforded constant work. From being the poorest man in his township, he became the richest, and purchased a cart and pony, which was also very much employed. So that, but for the mortality in his family, he would have done well. But, poor fellow! all his sons and daughters sickened as they grew up, and died away of consumption; and he, the last time I saw him, was a miserable object, just about to join them. Well, this poor Callum was the greatest night-coward I ever yet encountered. He never would come to his work in the morning, or go away home at night, without being accompanied by either son or daughter, or both; for this night-fear ran strong in the family, and the child that accompanied the father was obliged to have a companion to return home. The loss of labour that took place in the family owing to this insane fear was prodigious, for if he had no companion, he would sit up by the kitchen fire all night, and thus lose his next morning's work. We often talked and reasoned with him, but to no purpose. It was not that he was afraid of robbers, for there were no such things. He was not afraid of ghosts; but it was simply an indescribable terror of being by himself in the dark, and I believe but for this terror, he would have been the richest man in his district—nay, more; he was watcher over my river at Saxay, and, in company with another, would go out at night, and was really a very fair watcher, for he understood the ways of fish, and the ways of their enemies; and though I don't suppose he would have risked his bones in a row, yet he counteracted poaching.

Now when I instance Callum as an example of night fear, it is not describing him alone.

Very, very few are devoid of it, and there was a peculiar spot not far from me which was the dread of the whole country. It was a rock on the road to Stornoway, said to be haunted by the ghost of a boy murdered there some years ago, the particulars of which I shall here relate.

In days of yore, two boys of Stornoway, instead of going to school, amused themselves with going out egg-stealing in the grouse-hatching time. They quarrelled about the division of the spoil, and one of the young gentlemen hit the other rather too hard on the head with a stone and killed him. He was horridly frightened; but when he found his companion dead, he kept his wits, and dug a hole in the muir under this rock by the burnside, in which he buried the body. He then betook himself to Harris, got on board a fishing-boat in Tarbet, whence he made his way to the mainland, became a sailor, and wandered about the world for many years. At last, in the course of his voyages, the ship—in which, I think, he had become mate—went into the port of Stornoway for repairs. When there, instigated by an almost supernatural anxiety and curiosity, he went on shore. He could find no traces of the cabins where his own family and that of his poor friend used to live; and he entered one of those small public eating and drinking-houses which were always, I presume, open for the refreshment of sailors, and called for something to eat. While his food was preparing, his attention was drawn to something peculiar in the shape of the handles of the knife and fork laid on the table; and he was examining them closely when his hostess addressed him, "You may well look at those handles; for we got them in a strange way. I was returning home one evening from Balallan with a hay-load, and sat down by the burnside at the bottom of the hill near the white rock, when my eyes were attracted by something white under the rock, and, in what seemed to have been a hole, I found three or four bones of dead sheep, I suppose, and I brought them home with me and made handles for two or three of my old knives that wanted them. But, mon! what's the matter with your hands? they are full of blood." The sailor sprang to his feet with a wild scream. "They're no sheep's banes, they're poor Willie's banes, and I am his murderer, and see how they tell the truth and witness against me." For it was the bones, and not his hands, that were oozing with blood. He at once confessed his crime, was tried, condemned, and executed on Gallows Hill, protesting to the last that he never had any ill-will to poor Willie, but only killed him in a fit of passion; but that he deserved his fate for not giving himself up at once and confessing the deed.

Ever since this occurrence this rock, under which the bones of the murdered Willie were found, was considered to be haunted. And the strange part of the story was that no one ever saw the ghost on the road to, but always on the road back from, Stornoway. Now, I am going to account for this. The rock was situated about four miles from Soval, on the right-hand side of the road, at the bottom of the hill, by a little stream. As you walked down the hill from Soval you saw nothing of the rock, because it was level with the heathy hill. As you walked down the hill upon this rock from Stornoway, it stood on the contrary—a bluff, bare, grey rock, white in part towards the top, as many of these rocks often are. At one time, for some years, I had to go into Stornoway regularly once a week, and, if the weather permitted me at all, I returned the same night —particularly in the woodcock season—if possible. Well, one horrid day, I had walked in, as the morning was Lewisian, and I wished to give old Fred a rest, as the next day we were bound for Dalbeg. My business over, I resisted the hospitable invitations of my friends, and started for Soval somewhere about eight or nine o'clock. It was a fine, bright moonlight night, after the wet morning; the wind had gone north, and I cracked on best pace for home, with a good caulker of the old Sheriff's excellent whisky. I was cheering myself with the thoughts of the cosy fireside at home, and anticipations of the woodcocks for the morrow, as, doing my four miles an hour, I swung down the hill beyond the five-mile stone, when I was pulled up all of a heap; for lo! there, on the haunted rock, stood a boy in a shirt! The boy's ghost! I had passed, some half-mile behind me, two or three people on the road, or I think I should have bolted. Instead of this, helped with the Sheriff's caulker, I walked on. The ghost disappeared. This seemed odd, and knowing people were behind me, I got very bumptious, and turned back to have another look: when, as I got back, I saw not the whole, but half the ghost, and then presently no ghost at all; and then there was not the same clear brightness as before, and for a few seconds the moon wept behind a cloud over some fair maid's misfortunes; then it broke forth again, slowly, to shine upon a very small bit of ghost indeed. By this time, hearing voices, I became very valiant, and distinctly saw the ghost become bigger. "Hang it!" thinks I to myself. "Maidens may love the moon, or the Buffalo gals like to come out and dance by its light; but I never heard of a ghost's partiality to its cold, pale rays;" and I took a very steady look, and then I found out exactly what the ghost was. In the angle I was coming down the road, the moon just struck upon the white part of the rock I have already alluded to, and it did appear something like a figure; and I can perfectly understand any one, seeing what I saw, being awfully scared; I know I was, and I don't to this hour understand why I did not run away, and certain sure I am I should have done so but for the above-mentioned reasons. The good people came up very shortly, and were astonished at catching me up. I thought I might do them some good by explaining and pointing out to them what I had seen, and thus diminishing the awe of the spot. Not a bit of it; I did more harm than good. In vain I tried to walk my best the rest of the way to Soval. They stuck to me like leeches, and would not leave my kitchen fire till light came; and the ghost story was for ever confirmed. As sure as death, the master had seen and spoken to the ghost, and there was no mistake, and I was implored not to go night-walking any more; and because I was obliged to do so sometimes, I believe they conceived no very good opinion of me, but thought that I was no that canny as it behoved a man to be, who had once seen a ghost and talked to it, and then ganged the same gait. It was just a warning, and it would fare worse with me if I did not heed.

CHAPTER XIX.

M'AULAY'S STORIES.

MURDOCH M'AULAY was not only a good stalker, boatman, and right-hand man, but he was altogether quite a character. Born in Harris, he believed there was no such a country in the world, and he rather looked down on the Lews. His family had been foresters for generations under the McLeods, and afterwards under the Dumore family, who came in after the McLeods. He was fond of the old stocks; and, if the truth must be spoken, had no sort of reverence, respect, or love for any but the old stock. He looked upon all purchasers of Highland property as men who had acquired their property unjustly; and I believe he would at any time readily have joined in any raid to turn them out again. I can understand it, for the bodies one sees now in possession of some of the old Highland properties are not lovable specimens of humanity, and seem utterly out of their places when attempting to do Highlander. In addition to these peculiarities, he was a great relator of stories, and he always prefaced them by saying—"A man once told me, but I don't believe him," though he firmly did, and a great deal more too.

We were stalking together in Carneval, over Loch Lewid, one very fine day, and he pointed out to me a very small island on it, which had been the scene of a very queer story. There was a man who many years ago used to stalk this hill very much, and he was a very bad man, and never cared what day he went out. He was stalking once, and it was on the Sunday, and he had inveigled out with him a friend not quite so bad as himself—one who for worlds would not have shot a stag on the Sabbath himself, but who, at the same time, would not have had the slightest objection to partake of one shot on that holy day. They had been a long weary way, and, at last, very tired, sat down to have a wee bit luncheon and a dram, and a smoke, by the side of Loch Langavat, opposite a small island not very far out. To their surprise, in the middle of their smoke, they both saw a large, full royal lying down comfortably on the island, which they must have been blind not to have perceived before. The bad man took his rifle, loaded it, and swam away for the island, never losing sight of his stag; when, lo! on his landing, and getting to the spot on which he had seen it, it was gone. He swam to shore very savage, and abused his friend for his bad watching—when he positively declared he had never seen the beast move, and there it was still, and he pointed to it lying in exactly the same attitude and spot in which it was first seen. Bad man then re-swam to the island with exactly the same success as the first time; and returned the second time more savage than ever with his friend, who, however, again pointed out to him this singular stag in the same spot. Nowise daunted, this desperate man swore he would not be foiled, and prepared for the third time to return to the island. His friend in vain implored him not to try any more, that the beast was "no canny," and that evil would come of this third attempt: but no—wilful man must have his way, and this man swore a frightful oath that he would have that stag, or that stag should have him. According he swam out the third time; and, as he reached the island, his friend saw the stag rise, and walk quietly on towards the place where the stalker would land—viz.: the far-off side of the island—till he disappeared over the crest of the hill. Long did that man wait for his bad friend, but he never returned.

"And what became of him, M'Aulay?"

"I do not know, I do not believe the story; but he was a very bad man." He believed every word of it.

He had another story of Glenvicadale, the first glen in Harris, just after you pass the stream that runs up it, and which gives it its name. This is a very pretty little brook, which, when there is much water in it, is a very rattling stream. Many a pleasant day have I passed by its banks, catching brown and small sea-trout. At its head, about two miles up the glen, is a diminutive loch — you might almost call it a pond, so surrounded is it everywhere with sedge that the water is not to be got at for it. Out of this small lochie, said to be unfathomable, runs the river—and it is this spot that is the scene of one of M'Aulay's traditions.

About a mile above this loch—which was once supposed to be much larger—is a very large rock, in which is a great cavern, with a natural wall so running across in front of it, that a few bars of wood and planks could at any time convert it into a comfortable temporary abode for a night or so. In former days, when deer-stalkers were not so particular about their accommodation, many an old chief of those parts made this cavern his resting place. Once upon a time, then, a tired deer-stalker betook himself, with his two deer-hounds, to this shelter for the night. In those days the deerhound was always the faithful companion of the deer-stalker; and sorry indeed am I that the custom was ever given up, for the deerhound is a noble beast—and when really made the companion of man, for whom of all dogs he is the most fitted from his sagacity and attachment, is the best. Besides, bringing the stag to bay with two good hounds is the best part of deer-stalking. Well, after, of course, eating and drinking, our stalker and his hounds were sitting by the fire, winking and dozing as bipeds and quadrupeds generally do after a hard day's walking—a tremendous knocking at the door was heard. I suppose, had he lived in our times, our tenant of the cavern would have sung, "Who's that knocking at the door, Miss Dinah?" But he was not up to this, so, like a bold forester as he was, he opened the door—when, lo! before it stood an enormous monster, armed, of course, with a big club, who demanded who dared intrude thus and take possession of his castle? My stalker, being a man of quick impulse and presence of mind, answered not, but set his hounds at the monster. Accustomed to stags' antlers, they cared little for an unarmed head, and at the monster they went, who did not act up to the savagery of his appearance, but fairly turned tail and fled at an awful pace in the direction of the wee bit lochie. Into this he jumped with a terrible bound and demoniac yell, the hounds fastening on him as he sprang. Long did the master wait for the appearance of his faithful dogs. But nothing was ever seen or heard of monster or hound. It is supposed to be unfathomable, this loch, and occasionally in the calmest of weather to be most violently agitated, and to froth black. This is the effect of the monster and the hounds struggling every now and then to lose their hold and come to the surface, which they can't, of course. It is full of fish, which never are to be captured. Such was M'Aulay's story, which he said he did not believe, either. I dispelled the charm, as far as catching fish went, by getting a little coble to it one day, when I got the most frightful midging I ever in my days, even in the Lews, experienced, and caught only a sea-trout or two; but did not ever try it again, for the simple reason that the game was not worth the candle.

But there was another story of that stout henchman that beat them all. He was stalking in the park one day, before we took the Aline shooting, with a former tenant. They had never been able to spy any stag that they thought worth shooting; and, towards the afternoon, they sat down to luncheon rather disconsolate. While discussing this meal, they were all of a sudden astonished by a little old man in a grey coat joining them unawares, his approach not having been perceived. He sat down a little way from them, looking wistfully at the bread and cheese. They took him for one of the park shepherds, though wondering at not knowing him by sight even. With true Highland hospitality, they tendered him of their fare, of which he greedily and gratefully, but silently, partook. Whisky, to their very great astonishment indeed, he refused. After the usual pipe they resumed their stalking, never noticing the disappearance of their little old friend in the grey coat; but he was gone, and nobody saw him go. Very shortly afterwards they found a stag with a very odd, queer head, and, apparently, a good body—just the sort of beast to set a stalker's heart on fire. At him they went with a will; and, after a long, hard stalk, got up to him and killed him. They found him to be a very old stag indeed, with a head denoting great age, and a very large, but thin body. M'Aulay never remembered seeing this head before, and such a forester as he was could not have ever seen this head and not remember it. But, at any rate, there he was, and a very curious beast, well worth the trouble he had given. They bled him, they gralloched him, and in his stomach they found the bread and cheese ! ! !

Murdoch M'Aulay was a wonderful stalker, and rather a wag about it, as the following story will prove. For some time before shootings and forests became what they are now—so dear that none but very rich gentlemen and cotton lords, *et hoc genus omne*, can look at them, both Harris and Lewis were much neglected, and there was a great deal of quiet poaching of deer going on. There was one—I won't mention his name, for he was a great friend of mine, though now dead, and recollections may be unpleasant, and so we will call him Donald—who was a very good stalker; and, his farm or holding being near where deer lived, and he fond of venison, sometimes helped himself to some. One day he had set his heart upon a particularly fine stag, which he was getting up to well. It happened, though rather unluckily for him, that Murdoch M'Aulay was stalking the identical same beast, and, during the operation, he descried our friend Donald and his similar pursuit. A thought struck Murdoch—to drop stalking the stag, and stalk Donald instead. He instantly put his thought in practice, and very successfully. Donald had just got to his stone, or lump, or knoll, handy for a shot at his prey, and was taking his last anxious peer over its top to ascertain his stag's exact position, and, for that purpose, had done what all stalkers do—laid his rifle cannily by his side, convenient to his right hand. Alongside this spot ran a sort of burn or watercourse, at this time all but dry, into which M'Aulay had wormed himself, and while Donald was making his last observations, quietly lifting his hand he abstracted the rifle, and retreated down the burn again. Satisfied with his position and that of the stag, our stalker felt for his weapon, when, to his horror, it responded not to his touch, and, lo! it was gone; and, after a few seconds of great suspense, a deep, sepulchral voice sounded from the depths of the earth, "Donald, whare's your rifle?" Horrified, Donald sprang to his feet, regardless of deer, or anything but that he was bewitched, and ran for his life, never stopping till he reached his own cabin-door.

CHAPTER XX.

MY FIRST WILD BOAR.

WHEN I was a cheery boy of some seventeen or eighteen—and that is a long time ago—I was passing a long vacation in that, alas! now no longer, most charming of all places, Paris. My old and dear friend, General, afterwards Duc, de St. Simon, was ordered into Brittany, to inspect some cavalry regiments. I was wild to go with him, for he was a keen and good sportsman, a fine rider, a good shot, a gallant soldier, and a thorough French gentleman of the old régime. Brittany was then famed for its sports, and I knew how my friend would employ his non-inspecting days. He was willing to take me; but how? was the question. His travelling calèche only held himself and his aide-de-camp, and he laughingly said that the only way would be to ride with his faithful servant and courier, Aimée; but that was too much for me, particularly at that time of the year. This put me upon my mettle, and I swore go I would, if I dropped.

Accordingly, one fine evening in August, 1818, we started. I have lived to see leathers in and out twice. At that time they were just going out, and were worn bright yellow. I had brought a pair with me from Cambridge, and top-boots. I had a good English saddle, but foolishly did not take my English bridle, or rather reins. I had a good pair of spurs, and a French postilion's whip, out of which, however, I never could extract the true invigorating "clack-clack." Merrily did we clatter up the Champs Elysées. Every one knew St. Simon, and having lived a good deal as a boy in Paris, I had no small acquaintance, and many were the kindly greetings we had from happy faces that were enjoying the evening air. It was very well for the first twenty-five leagues (and we had eighty-eight to do), as the horses were good, and the French bidet de poste was then, as he still is, very pleasant in his ambling canter. But as you got further, things changed for the worse. There was nothing but the common posters to ride, and my friend Aimée, an old soldier, managed to get the best always. The nags wanted a little hand now, and I felt the want of my English reins. I remember thinking the post-reins iron, not leather, and towards six or seven in the morning it was positive pain to hold them. For all that, during the whole eighty-eight leagues I got but two falls—one as I pulled up on a lovely evening to look at the fair town of Alençon, when my horse gently paid his devotions to mother earth (in admiration of the scene also, I suppose), rising quickly again; the other, in passing through a small town, when my horse blundered on to his head from being driven into the gutter by a market cart. Now, I do not think one could have ridden the same distance on English posters with the same result.

My hands hurt me then a good deal, but that was the only damage I felt; but I cannot say that about ten o'clock in the morning—the last post we were to ride before breakfast—I did not contemplate with some disgust a very sorry-looking, raw-boned stallion that was brought out to me, with heavy shoulders, groggy legs, and unmistakable knees. I could not help uttering my complaints to a merry-eyed Norman lass that was standing by, and who turned out to be the postmaster's daughter. Whether she pitied the horse or me I don't know, but she told me that if I promised to take great care of him she would lend me " le bidet de papa;" and out came an uncommonly nice grey pony, with capital action, who went his two posts rather faster than papa's usual pace; and then the luxury of the toilet at the end of that post, and after that the delicious *déjeûner à la fourchette* and a good rest.

I started again as fresh as a fly, forgetting my hands; and with the exception of the halt for supper, rode merrily through the night. By this time I was up to my friend Aimée, and I managed also in passing through some town to buy a bridle, à l'Anglaise, with enormous buckles, and though it was not the sort of thing I should have liked to have turned out with his Grace of Beaufort's hounds at Stanton Park, it was a wonderful relief after the posting bridles. Then I learnt the courier's trick of getting a good start of the carriage, clattering along two or three posts quick, taking a rest. Reader, if you want to know luxury, ride courier for a night or two, get a good start of an hour of your carriage, and then, when you reach the end of the post, give orders to have your horse all ready to start the moment the carriage comes up, and throw yourself into the masses of straw that fill some of the stalls. If you don't enjoy that snooze, you have never tasted true rest.

And thus we cantered on through the second night. I don't tell you that towards the second morning I should not have enjoyed the carriage more than the saddle; but I had said I would do it, and was determined to stick to it. Besides, it is wonderful how one learns to doze on horseback. The good French breakfast—and such coffee!—set me quite up, and right merrily did I ride into Rennes (our first place of inspection) that afternoon. How I enjoyed my warm bath and bed after that long, hot ride, which still I look back to as one of the pleasantest in my life, save and except a canter to the Rock to meet the dear old Kilkenny hounds in the olden time, when that prince of huntsmen and riders, Johnnie Power, hunted them; and poor Richard Cox, and the two Baileys, and the Stannards, and the Quins, and the Montgomerys, and that hardest of pill-boxes, Dr. O'Reilly, rode to them.

How I found it out I don't know, but I did that evening—that there was some good shooting in the neighbourhood of Rennes. I knew that everything would be open to the General; but as he must first look after his cavalry, I was determined not to lose a day. The shooting had not been opened by the préfet of the department, I had no *porte d'armes*, I had no permission from any one, and I did not know one field from another; but I had my gun and poor Die —old Tom's ancestress, then about nine or ten months old—and off I started early the next morning, violating every law, human and divine, for it was Sunday. But this, I fear, I calculated on; for the Breton peasants were then, as they are now, very devout, and were sure to be at church most of the day, and I was more afraid of them than anything else. I cannot say I did much execution; for I could hardly hit a haystack flying. The day was intensely hot. It was nearly Die's first essay, and though the corn was cut, the buckwheat was not; and into that I dared not (except when the coast was quite clear) intrude, for fear of a drubbing from the peasants, which I should have assuredly got, as I deserved. I got three or four partridges, and about as many quails. But, oh, what stubbles! I have never seen such, before or since. High and dirty! would that the world abounded in such, and that I could live and shoot where the worst farming existed! Towards the afternoon I met a French chasseur, marauding like myself. At first we were inclined to fly each other; but we fraternized, and, thanks to him, I got safe back to Rennes without encountering any gardes champêtres or gendarmes, which otherwise I probably might have done. He had a very decent, queer-looking dog, who trotted not faster than we walked, but with a capital nose, and a dead hand at catching a hare on her form; and we had, during the time I spent at Rennes, some little private poaches of our own on bye-days, when we always got something.

When I got home I caught it from the General for my exploits, but my not returning quite empty-handed mollified him a little; for he was an uncommon poacher himself. Also, he had not much time to scold, as there was a grand dinner and ball at the Préfecture, for which there was barely time to dress. Don't cry out, gentle reader. This was forty-five years ago, and I was barely eighteen, and dinners and balls on Sundays were then the rule, not the exception, abroad. Moreover, I think the world was not a bit more wicked then than now. As the English friend of the General, I was nearly as much a lion as himself that night. My ride from Paris and shooting exploit of the morning — which every one assured me ought to have sent me to prison — made the good people of Rennes think me madder than Englishmen in general. I could speak French perfectly, and sing and dance well then: so I sang duets with Madame la Préfete, who screamed most discordantly; danced with the daughters, who were not beauties; and, with the help of the General, so ingratiated myself with the Préfet, that he promised me a *porte d'armes*, and all his interest in procuring shooting as soon as it was opened, which it was to be in a day or two. I thus soon found myself in clover. I shot where I had leave, and poached where I had none. I missed a great many partridges, red and grey quails, and hares, and snipes; but then I was young, and had time to learn. In the dragoon regiment the General was inspecting there were some very nice young fellows; and between shooting and balls and dinners and plays, merrily went the time.

At last the neck of the inspection was broken, and a *grande partie de chasse* was arranged to come off in a royal forest some eight or nine leagues from Rennes. We started one fine morning in such a carriage, with four such long-tailed horses, and such a coachman with such a cocked hat, and such a pigtail! I thought I should have choked. We ambled gracefully along, a little slower than we could have walked, and arrived about eleven in the centre of the forest—a place something like the Horse-guards in the Cirencester Woods, only nothing near so fine. Here were assembled a motley crew of chasseurs, dogs, and piqueurs. There was one of the sportsmen particularly attracted my attention, and who attached himself to me at once. He examined all my accoutrements, and found a singular fault with my gun—viz., that the locks were bad, because the cocks did not go far back enough, and consequently had not sufficient play, or force, to strike the hammers hard enough to give good fire. No reasoning I possessed could make my friend understand that the goodness of a lock depended on the proper balancing of the springs. These were flint-and-steel days, remember. But don't laugh at my friend—whom I shall call Carabine; he was a thorough and enthusiastic sportsman, and such a walker I never saw in my life! I think his legs could not have been flesh and bone and muscles and sinews; they surely were catgut and wire. He seemed hardly to touch the ground. He had walked that morning from Rennes; he walked the forest all day at the heels of the hounds; and what he did shall be seen at its close.

The guns lined one of the alleys down-wind, and the forest, or different quarters of it, were beaten up to them by the hounds and piqueurs. I was committed to Carabine's care, to be posted in a remote corner, in case anything went back, with directions to move on towards the posted guns as the hunt (as we used to say in Ireland) came on. I trotted at Carabine's heels till he left me, nearly blown, by a tree, which he charged me not to leave till I heard his double Chouan whistle. Did you ever hear one? The railway is a joke to it. He then plunged into the wood. All was still for a long time. At last I heard the cry of hounds. It approached, and I really thought I was in for a shot; but, whether from over-keenness I showed, or did something I ought not to have done, the hounds turned, and I soon heard an unearthly something, twice repeated, that made me jump, and down my cross-ride I went, best pace, for the great alley, parallel to which, apparently, the hounds were running. As I came in sight of the first gun, I recognised Aimée, who was chasseur as well as courier and valet. I halted, for the hounds, having turned, were running towards us, and I felt sure that the beast afoot, whatever it was, would break between Aimée and myself. Just then, what should spring into the alley—evidently only disturbed, not hunted —but a little, miserable roe-deer calf. Immediately I looked down Aimée's barrels, loaded, one with buck-shot, the other with two balls! Grimaldi never threw a back somersault quicker than I did into the wood, as I felt a most uncomfortable whistling of all sorts of things just over the spot I had so hastily left. Though I heard the hounds coming very close, I did not move for a second or two, expecting Aimée's second barrel, both of which, however, had gone at once. I jumped up in time, not to see, but to hear, something disappear in the thick wood on the opposite side of the alley, after which I fired. Presently the hounds appeared, and crossed, and, immediately after them, Carabine. I was interrogated, but could give no account of what had passed. It might have been the Wild Huntsman, for aught I know. The rest of the party congregated immediately. Aimée was blown up for firing at the poor little calf, which, of course, he had missed, and nearly bagged me. But, oh, dear! how they pitched into and laughed at me! "L'Anglais! l'Anglais! to have left his place just as the beast was breaking, and not to know even what it was!" Carabine scowled at me, the General was ashamed of me, the young dragoons chaffed me till I felt inclined to fight them all round.

In jumps Carabine into the wood, and returns at once with the intelligence that the animal is a wolf, that the hounds would follow him all day, or for a month, as they never like running up to one of those animals, who, therefore, never troubles himself with going too fast. But the worst was that our sport was spoilt for the day, as the only chance of recovering the hounds was for Carabine to head them some three leagues off by making a short cut through the forest. Disconsolately, therefore, did we wend our way back to the place where the carriage was to meet us, I with my tail very much between my legs.

We had barely time for a little luncheon, when, just as the horses were putting to, up comes Carabine with the hounds, having recovered them just where he intended to do. Having taken a small glass of brandy and a morsel of bread, he was about to return on foot to Rennes, when I insisted he should have my place in the carriage. I fear there was little real charity in my offer. I wanted to get away from my companions, who were driving me half wild. Not a bit of it. I could not stand the walk, &c., &c. At last he said he would sit on a sort of bar that was at the back of the undercarriage of our conveyance. We declared he would be shaken to death in a quarter of a league, which he would have been. At last he spied my saddle, which Aimée had smuggled into the carriage, thinking he might have to ride in the course of the day. How Carabine managed I don't know to this day; but he put my saddle on the aforesaid bar, mounted, stuck his feet in the stirrups, and thus rode, as he said, most comfortably into Rennes. There was a dinner with the colonel of the regiment that day, and a ball; but I did not dare face it, and slunk to bed.

Next day, Carabine came to see the General, and, to console me, he said he had arranged an extraordinarily fine *partie de chasse* in another and a better forest, famous for its wild boars, which were reckoned the largest and most savage in Brittany. At first the General threatened to leave me at home, in punishment of my doings the day before, which, on reconsideration, turned out not so bad. On the contrary, up to the somersault, Carabine declared I had displayed a most innate knowledge of the noble science; and, moreover, as but for throwing myself into the wood, Aimée must have bagged me, he was for the future to be left at home, or, at any rate, not trusted with a gun.

At last the day was settled, and came off. We started, in a contrary direction to the day before, to another forest, some of the scenery of which was very beautiful. The ground was wild and undulating, with some very pretty streams running through it. It was a lovely day, and as we were now well into September, the excessive heat of a French August of those days had passed. Carabine still patronized me, and kept me to himself. He placed me by a pollard oak, on a bank that overhung a pretty, wild, rocky stream, where the trout were rising very fast. On the other side of the valley, partly wooded, partly open, through which the stream ran, was hilly ground, covered with brushwood, rock fern, and broom, very fair to look at. I could enjoy the landscape thoroughly, though my thoughts ran much on the boar, which Carabine assured me would be found; that if it was the celebrated, well-known one, he would be sure to run the hill and take the stream; that I must be sure not to miss him, or, at any rate, not to wound him, as if I did I might as well consider myself dead, as this very animal had killed a piqueur last year, and upset himself, fortunately without any injury. I inquired why I, an unfledged greenhorn, was selected, of all people, to face such a monster, and not the General, who was a real good shot and accustomed to such game. Carabine declared he was bent on giving me a chance of redeeming my character; that there I should stand, and nowhere else; and that if I missed!—he looked unutterable things—and away with him to the piqueurs and the hounds.

And here was I left, an unprotected babe in the woods, a long way from any one, to encounter the furious animal. I loaded my gun carefully, putting two balls, screwed together, in each barrel. I laid my gun against the tree, and sat me down to rest and gaze. After a long time, I heard a distant noise and cries. Gradually the note of hounds came nearer—nearer—nearer, till it seemed to reach the copse-hill before me. Once or twice I caught a glimpse of something coming through it, and at last saw it clearly—a beast of some sort. It broke, and lo! and behold! it was a kind of a bluish, brownish, slate-coloured animal, decidedly of the pig kind. It was not going very fast; it looked very hot, very fat, very sulky. It wended its way across the flat towards the stream, and, merciful powers! as if it was taking aim at the very tree under which I stood. I was very keen, but I was troubled in my mind. At last my gentleman, as he neared the water, diverged a little, took the stream, which he waded and swam across, giving two or three grunts, as if he found it refreshing. I then saw it was a boar—Meleager's own Calydonian never looked so savage. I felt his tusks already in my groin. I could have run away, but I didn't; so I clutched my gun, cocked both barrels, and awaited my foe with grim determination. Then, as he mounted the bank on which I stood, just as he was topping it, and his head and shoulders were over it, I blazed both barrels at once at him, dropped my gun, and hopped like a squirrel into my tree, thinking that, being a boar and not a bear, he could not climb after me.

All was still—as one of the songs of the day said,—

"Every leaf was at rest, and I heard not a sound."

Thinks I to myself, "If he meant mischief he would have turned by this time." I dropped out of my tree, crept cautiously on, expecting I don't know what. When, about fifteen yards off, lo! there lay the beast dead, all but the quivering of the limbs, with a large hole drilled in his body, as the four balls had gone in behind the shoulder and through him.

Don't think meanly of me, ye glorious

Indians! I was but a boy, and never had an opportunity of riding to hog, which even now I would give half a life were it to come over again to do. But I was very proud of my boar.

The hounds, who seemed to have no wish to come very near him, were now reaching the verge of the copse, with Carabine close at them. I caught glimpses of some of the guns moving, and set up the French "who—whoop"—hallali! hallali!—if my recollection of their terms of chase be right. The hounds quickened their pace, and with Carabine took the stream gallantly. St. Simon and the rest appeared. I was no longer a muffin, but the slayer of the famed boar of the forest. My luck was envied, my prowess and coolness extolled. I kept my own counsel.

And so fell my first wild boar; and though I have killed others, they never equalled that first.

CHAPTER XXI.

THE LATE DUKE DE ST. SIMON.

MY dear old friend the Duc de St. Simon lived to a great age, and died, a hale, hearty old man, some three or four years ago, and I don't think it amiss to record here a passage of his life well deserving his country's gratitude, and one or two anecdotes connected with him. In the autumn of 1815 a large portion of the Prussian army was quartered in Normandy, with the intention of occupying Cherbourg, then very slenderly garrisoned. Blücher, with his staff, was at Caen, the headquarters of the French military division commanded by St. Simon, then a young general of brigade. The Prussians, on their entry into Caen, demanded that the small force under his orders should lay down its arms. To such an unprovoked indignity—for this was in September, long after all hostilities had ceased— the man who had been Ney's aide-de-camp not only for two years in Spain, where the gallant Colbert fell by his side, but for several in Germany; who at Jena had cut his way through the Prussian hussars, carrying his marshal's orders, and was reported as dead in consequence of the wounds there received—refused obedience. But, unwilling that there should be any resort to force, which would probably have led to bloodshed, the young general signified his intention of parading his small force at a certain hour on the Place d'Armes, and then evacuating the town. This he accordingly did, and directed his troops to proceed to Cherbourg. He had already passed most of the troops in his division into that place, together with all disbanded soldiers passing through Caen from the army of the Loire and different other quarters. Thus, by the time the Prussians were ready to occupy Cherbourg, it was garrisoned with a good body of veteran troops, burning with hatred against them more than any of the Allies. They did not venture to force their way in, finding discretion the better part of valour. Thus backed, perhaps, a little by that pressure that saved the bridge of Jena, Cherbourg was preserved from the Prussians. The task, however, was difficult, for, had any collision taken place, the French

Government would not—possibly could not—have supported their general.

The Duc de St. Simon, then a colonel, was the officer who, accompanied by Colonel Cook, carried to Soult the news of the abdication of Napoleon, in 1814. Soult discredited, or pretended to discredit, the information, and proceeded to try St. Simon by a sort of court martial, and General Foy told me himself he voted for shooting him. Certainly he was sentenced to be shot; but whether through the kindness of Soult's staff, or by his directions, shortly after the sentence was announced to him an aide-de-camp came into the room, and, asking him if that was his horse under the window, left it immediately. St. Simon took the hint and made his escape to Suchet, with whom he had long served in Catalonia, where he was in safety.

It was either on his way from or back to Paris on this hazardous expedition, that the envoy and the ex-emperor on his road to Elba met at a post-house when changing horses. Napoleon, knowing him well, sent for him. The white cockade was in his shako, and St. Simon, with the instinct and the breeding of a thorough gentleman, with something, perhaps, of the galled pride of a soldier at thus entering his old emperor's presence, under whose leading and victorious eagles he had marched into many of the capitals of Europe, tried to keep the new cockade out of sight. "*Ah, vous en avez déjà honte!*" laughingly remarked Napoleon. St. Simon, who was as quick and ready a man as ever lived, told me he felt as if choked, and could not utter a word.

The British public will probably take little interest in this subject, but these reminiscences might find their way to France, and show how Englishmen can appreciate Frenchmen on public grounds. May I be permitted to add that, if such should be the case—if in that once fair, beautiful Paris, there should be still living one only that remembers us both—I would wish that one to know that I could not refrain from striving to pay this humble tribute to the memory of one with whom I passed some of the happiest days of youth, and to whose early kindness, wise counsel, and good example I owe a deep debt of gratitude.

CHAPTER XXII.

CONCLUSION.

IT is a good rule, I believe, to give up doing what you wish to do, provided it is not an absolute duty to do it; for if you err, you err on the safe side. Now, I am heart and soul in these wilds, and I believe I could find something to say about them as long as life lasts. Every day brings some fresh occurrence, creating some new idea. Above all, every day seems to sharpen up the memory of the past. As, then, I feel how bitter it is to tear myself away from a subject so dear to me; as each companion in these wild regions is recalled to my memory, how gladly would I say something of him as his shadow passes before me, and seems to hover about the spots endeared by some recollection!—as I feel all this, it makes me sad to think that the time is come when I must part with the shadow, as I have already parted with the substance. But it must be done. Were I a poet, how should I endeavour to describe what I so acutely feel? "The old man's occupation's gone." But there is a consolation still. Do you remember that great man's picture—great let me call him, for he painted, and paints, dogs as they are—Landseer's, "There's life in the old dog yet"? There is much that I still could say which might do in a book, but would not suit the columns of the *Field*, to whose editor, for his courtesy and kindness in allowing me scope to express my real feelings about the Lews, I take this public opportunity of returning my sincerest thanks. There are visions passing through the old man's brain, as old Whack lies dreaming and whining at his feet over the woodcocks on Dalbeg Hill, of, if time and opportunity permit, retouching and adding to these sketches till they attain the form of a book, and their writer going down to posterity as having written one; for "it is a very great performance," as a very clever woman once said to me, "to write a book at all, bad as it possibly may be." For the present, however, he feels, and with deep sorrow, that it is time to draw his mantle round him.

Before quitting the subject, however, allow

him to hang a little more upon it. Like the old hound, he will keep sniffing about a scent, still remembering how once he could throw his head to the wind and run it breast high.

It has been my endeavour in these reminiscences to give a thoroughly truthful and impartial account of a wild region—its *pros* and *cons*. Those as well acquainted with the country as myself tell me I have succeeded in doing so. I have written, too, with a sincere love for the Lews warming my heart, and the wish therefore to do it good. I feel bound to do so, not only in gratitude for the happy times spent there, but for the repeated acts of disinterested kindness received at the hands of many, many of its inhabitants. I believe I have left some friends, few enemies, in that country, and feel certain that if polled, the great majority of the Lewisians will do full justice to these Reminiscences and the spirit in which they are written. Of course, no one expects or wishes to please the whole world—nay, more, as some celebrity once said of another, "Thank God, he has always abused me!" and there may be, and no doubt are, those who are highly offended at the freedom of these Reminiscences. Of such the opinion is to me matter of the most supreme indifference. But even here the time will come when justice will be done and the ridiculous idea abandoned that the Reminiscences were undertaken with the view of "crabbing the Lews shooting." I entirely repudiate so unworthy an imputation, and am convinced the exact contrary will be their effect. Now, I will just tell a little Irish story of days of yore, and try to apply it here.

A long, long time ago, I was invited to a merry party at an Irish country-house, where was a great "gathering of the clans," for it was in the heart of the best part of the Kilkenny country, towards the close of the November meeting. We had a rattling run from Knockroe that day, and I arrived at my destination in bare time to dress for dinner. I was in high glee, for I was to ride my pet grey horse the next morning—the draw, Ballyspellan and the Rock. On the stairs I met our kind hostess, who, after the usual salutations, asked me whether I was hungry. I replied that I had been on horseback since six in the morning—it was now near that hour in the evening—done at least fifty (Irish) miles along the road, besides a very heavy run, and this upon one's biscuit and sherry-flask. "Very sorry for it, for it is unknown when we shall dine. Mr. B. was obliged to go to Dublin this morning, and the whole establishment is drunk." I reached my room, where I found my things ready to dress—only, my coat was before the fire, my dressing-gown laid out on the bed. I looked at my servant. He was steadily drunk. He was the best of men, passionately attached to his horses, a keen sportsman, and a good and daring horseman, with that rare gift—a light hand. Yet he never inquired about the hunt, or how his favourite Paddy had carried me; he did not trust himself to speak. Bad look-out, thought I to myself, as I dressed and repaired to the drawing-room. But who, when he entered that pleasantest of rooms, thought of anything but the merry, laughing, beautiful eyes, and the batch of pretty musical voices that were inquiring after the run, and where I came from last, and the particularly meaning inquiries about old John Downie's (my man's) health? Alas! but few of that joyous band are now left, though two are, I know, for I saw them last spring; and if this meets the eye of either —one, I know, reads *The Field*—let them send me some token they remember my tale. At no dinner-table I ever sat down to have I seen so many beautiful, happy faces ranged under its lights. One understood then the bashful Irishman asking the beautiful Duchess of Devonshire to let him light his pipe by the light of her eyes. And there sat our hostess —the merriest of that merry lot, handsomer even than her young, beautiful daughter—making the best of everything. The order of the table was strange—the waiting something wonderful: you got nothing you asked for, everything you did not want. Still our hostess never winced till, turning to her butler to beg him to interfere with a footman who showed symptoms of commencing a jig in the corner with Buttons, she saw her only stay lost, and she exclaimed, in an agony of despair, "Greaves, *you* are drunk!" That portly, old-fashioned functionary drew himself up to his full height, and, with consummate dignity, answered, in a clear, sonorous voice, "Mrs. B., I'm ashamed at your entertaining such mane ideas." This was too much, and I don't believe such a roar was ever heard at a civilized dinner-table before or since. I once dined at a large family party at my banker's in Berlin, where the dinner began at three and was not ended at eight, and at different intervals every male of the party, except myself, got up and kissed his neighbour. They were all hideous old women, such as Berlin alone can produce—for though it is the city of heroes, it is not the capital of beauties. How I did wish it had been the custom at our party! for my neighbour was "La Belle Sylvia," as we used to call her; and I never shall forget the ring of her voice or the laughter of her eyes at the butler's speech.

And now, to apply my story. To those, then, who, having known me for twenty years, must be aware that *noblesse oblige* forms some part of a gentleman's character, yet imagine that, from private pique, I would injure the beloved Lews, I say, "Mrs. B., I'm ashamed at you entertaining such mane ideas."

Let, then, these Reminiscences speak for themselves, and those capable of understanding them will say they are a proud justification, if, indeed, any was needed.

The mere shooter, who wants to let off his gun often, and do his grouse, his salmon, his deer, within a certain space of time, and get back to his partridges, his pheasants, and his early November hunting; or the man out only for a limited space of time—the man who don't like rough weather, rough country, rough work, or can't rough it—who is not fond of his dog, or don't understand him—who, above all things, can't find resource within himself—had best bide away from the Lews. But the true and genial lover of one of God's greatest gifts—the beauties of the wilderness, and being allowed to roam unmolested through them—this biped, who is thus three parts bred a hunter of wild things; who, of course, loves his dog as part of himself, and therefore understands him, and daily learns a great deal *from*, in his intercourse *with*, him; but which said biped can, if occasion need, sit for days inside the bothy when the weather won't let him go outside; let such biped eschew the world for some half the year, pitch his tent in these wilds, and he will be repaid.

I have, as I believe I have said before, shot grouse on the moss of Monaltree; killed woodcocks in all the wild coverts of the three Killarney lakes, on Turk Mountain, and in Mucross; snipes in the old Cambridgeshire and Norfolk fens, in the bog of Allen, and the shaky swamps of the Rhine; I have killed fish in most of the best rivers in Scotland, Wales, and Ireland, and white trout in Galway and Kerry; but give me a ten years' lease of life, a fresh pair of legs, my old team of Gordons, with Tom and Jock and Whack in the pride of their youth, and the Long Island for me against them all.

THE END.

www.ingramcontent.com/pod-product-compliance
Lightning Source LLC
Chambersburg PA
CBHW032111230426
43672CB00009B/1700